Before you
build

A step-by-step guide to extensions and renovations

Peter Chilvers, David Hill and Julian Owen

RIBA ✛ Publishing

Before You Build
A step-by-step guide to extensions and renovations

Peter Chilvers, David Hill and Julian Owen

© RIBA Enterprises, 2007

Published by RIBA Publishing, 15 Bonhill Street, London EC2P 2EA

ISBN 978 1 85946 185 3

Stock code 55695

British Library Cataloguing in Publications Data
A catalogue record for this book is available from the British Library.

Publisher: Steven Cross
Commissioning editor: John Elkington
Editor: The Creative Mix
Editorial project management and design: The Creative Mix
Printed and bound by: Latimer Trend, Plymouth
Photographs by: Julian Owen

RIBA Publishing is part of RIBA Enterprises Ltd. www.ribaenterprises.com

Cover photograph © Laurence Dutton/Getty Images

Every effort has been made to contact copyright holders. Queries should be addressed to RIBA Publishing, 15 Bonhill Street, London EC2P 2EA.

About the Authors

Peter Chilvers FRICS MBEng is a Chartered Building Surveyor who worked for many years in Building Control witnessing work to people's homes. Nowadays Peter works for PRP Architects.

David Hill has worked in construction for as long as he can remember. His career started in building control although today he runs his own private surveying practice where he operates as a claims investigator and loss adjuster for several insurance companies. David has been a past president of the District Surveyors Association and policy advisor to the Local Government Association. Today he works part time for the Federation of Master Builders and writes regularly for the Masterbuilder publication. David is Chairman of the local Chamber of Trade in his spare time and can be contacted via davidhill@fmb.org.uk.

Julian Owen MBE RIBA is an architect who has been helping people build and improve their homes for many years. He has written magazine articles and regularly delivered seminars at exhibitions on the subject of improving, designing and constructing homes. He runs his own practice in the East Midlands, and is currently chair of ASBA, the architects' network that he founded with his colleague, Adrian Spawforth, in 1993. He can be contacted through his website: www.julianowen.co.uk

The ASBA Architects' Network

a$\mathcal{S}$ba

ASBA is a national network of chartered architects set up by architect Julian Owen and others to provide cost-effective advice to people who wish to build or make alterations to their home. The network is a non-profit making company run by some of the practices that make up a membership that is spread across the whole of the UK and Northern Ireland. All ASBA architects are Chartered – that is members of the Royal Institute of British Architects who abide by RIBA training requirements and the RIBA code of conduct.

To find your local ASBA Architect, who can help with everything including feasibility advice, planning and building regulations applications, finding builders and inspecting the work on site, either visit the ASBA website www.asba-architects.org or dial freephone 0800 387310. Julian Owen, the ASBA Chair, can be contacted at www.julianowen.co.uk.

Contents

If you want to make alterations to your home, or even build a completely new house, this book will get you off to a flying start. It will arm you with the crucial information that you need to manage your project – from drawing up a brief, choosing a designer, preparing and negotiating local authority approvals, to choosing and managing a building contractor on site. It has been written by an experienced building control officer, who has spent many years inspecting building work, a surveyor, and an architect, who has designed and managed hundreds of extensions and conversions to private houses. It follows the steps that you need to take to see your project through to successful completion.

Architect-designed new house.

Preparing a project – flow chart of the process you will need to go through before you build

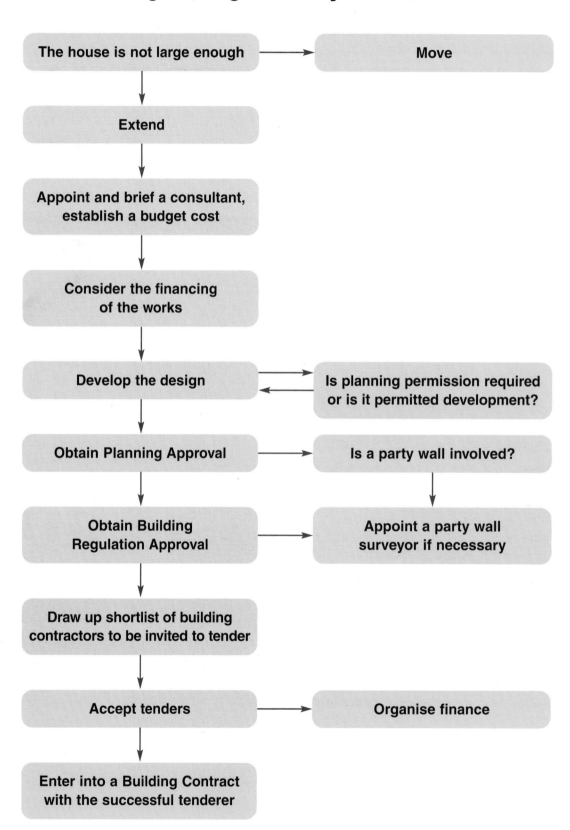

| The house is not large enough | → | Move |

Extend

Appoint and brief a consultant, establish a budget cost

Consider the financing of the works

| Develop the design | ⇄ | Is planning permission required or is it permitted development? |

| Obtain Planning Approval | → | Is a party wall involved? |

| Obtain Building Regulation Approval | → | Appoint a party wall surveyor if necessary |

Draw up shortlist of building contractors to be invited to tender

| Accept tenders | → | Organise finance |

Enter into a Building Contract with the successful tenderer

Space in the roof can be utilised to make one of the most cost-effective improvements to your home.

Should you move instead?

Altering your home is a major project. Before you launch into it, it is worth compiling a list of the disadvantages as well as the advantages. After this exercise you may decide that it's not worth the time, cost and hassle, and the best answer is to move house instead.

It's essential to consider both the **cost** and the **benefits.** Once the work is complete, the market value of your house should have increased – but will that increase be greater than the money you have spent on the project? If so, then you have made yourself a profit, although it is only 'on paper' until you sell up. For example, a loft conversion might cost £30,000, but the resulting extra bedroom and bathroom might add £40,000 to the value of the house – a profit of £10,000. But if the cost of the work is more than the house's increase in value, you effectively lose money. So adding a conservatory might cost £25,000 but add only £10,000 on to the value

A conservatory is a simple way of adding more living space.

of the house – a loss of £15,000.

The truth is that most home improvements will not make a profit: the main aim is not to make money, but to improve the lives of the occupants.

As well as the cost, there is the disruption and hassle of accommodating builders in your home for the duration of the construction – unless you are lucky enough to have somewhere else to stay until it is finished.

Preparing to start

The success – or failure – of your project depends on you. Your fate is usually decided well before work actually starts on site, so to be sure of success you need to do your homework properly.

First, you must set a realistic **budget.** Unfortunately, alterations to existing houses are notoriously difficult to estimate, particularly at the early stages. You don't have enough information to work out a price, and when you ask for quotes you are likely to be dealing with small builders, who all have their own ways of calculating their costs – from working out an accurate price and adding a margin based on how much they want the work, to nothing more than making a good guess. If you get a builder around in the early stages, they often can't give you a budget that is accurate enough to be useful. If you insist on a figure, it is likely to be optimistically low, because – assuming they want the work – they won't want to sound expensive and be left out later on.

If there are other properties in your area that have had work similar to your own plans, see if the owner is happy to discuss

A typical two-storey extension.

Table 1 Typical stages for a two-storey extension	
Stage	Typical time
Project preparation by homeowner	1–4 weeks
Drawing up a brief by homeowner	2–4 weeks
Finding an architect	2–3 weeks
Waiting for architect to be available	2–4 weeks
Preparing planning drawings	4–8 weeks
Planning process	8 weeks
Preparing Building Regulations drawings	4–6 weeks
Preparing tender package	1–2 weeks
Tendering process	3–4 weeks
Waiting for builder to be available	5–10 weeks
Building contract period	10–20 weeks
Total	**42–73 weeks**

the costs with you. Provided you allow something for inflation by the time you get on site, and you can compare their standard of work with what you're aiming for, then this is probably the closest you can get. It's worth having a quick chat with an architect or similar professional, who may be able to suggest a range of prices, but right at the start of the project the best you can do is make your own educated guess.

When you are estimating costs, try to include everything, not just the immediately obvious. Will you have to have other work done to the house? What about finance costs? Local authority fees? Consultants' fees? Landscaping costs? Finally, don't forget to allow for VAT. Most construction professionals exclude it when quoting costs, but it is usually paid on house alterations, and must be included if the builder is VAT registered.

Next you need to think about **financing** your project. Unless you have sufficient savings, and are happy to spend them, then once you have chosen a price range you need to check that your building society or bank is – in principle – prepared to increase your loan.

Now you have to work out a **timescale.** As

with the budget, project times can vary widely. The main factor here is the size and complexity of the design, but the build time can also be affected by things such as planning restrictions – and by the availability of builders. A typical two-storey side extension can easily take 12 months, from the time that you decide to proceed to the day that you take possession of the new rooms. A build programme of 15–20 weeks is not unusual. It helps to write out target dates for each stage, even if many of the time periods are guesses. You can update it as you get through each stage, and as your knowledge increases.

The next step is to put together a **project brief.** Most architects will tell you that a design is only as good as the brief that was prepared for it. You will probably work on the fine-tuning of your brief later on, with the help of your designer, but you can start the process off from day one by deciding on your basic requirements and *writing them down.* That last step is essential, especially if there are several family members affected. Compiling a record helps you to organise your thoughts; it also helps you to communicate them to everyone else, and to make sure that any disagreements are

Table 2 A typical brief for an extension	
Budget:	£50,000–£60,000 plus VAT
Extra space needed for:	Kitchen: twice as big, to have an American-style fridge and space for a four-person dining table. Also to have patio doors onto the garden, and get plenty of sunlight. Cloaks/WC 2 or 3 sq m bigger than existing. Garage, single car, built onto side of house, with access to hall.
New rooms needed:	Bedroom, reasonably sized double, new master bedroom. Bedroom, compact single, to act as study to get good daylight levels. En-suite bathroom, WC, shower, wash-hand basin; can be very compact.
Preferred location for extension:	Back of house, away from neighbours' houses and boundary.
Appearance:	To match in with existing house in scale and materials. Traditional design.
Future:	Allow for attic conversion at a later date.
Work to existing house:	New boiler. Redecorate hall, landing and all new rooms. Replace all existing timber windows with new to match.
Other important considerations:	House will be occupied during work, so kitchen will have to be kept working most of the time. A baby is due in 7 months' time so building work should not start until several weeks afterwards. We hate: dormer windows, concrete tiles, stripped pine and the colour green. We do not get along with the neighbour on one side of the house. We are in a conservation area (i.e. special planning controls).

raised and dealt with. It does not have to be a formal typed list – it could be a series of notes and sketch plans, or even written in marker pen on the family noticeboard, with each family member using a different colour.

There are many different ways to prepare a brief, and the contents will vary according to the people involved, and their tastes. For example, the simplest brief might be: 'Make our kitchen bigger and nicer.' But what does this mean? What about the size, location, cost and design of the extension? Perhaps you could even make the kitchen bigger by incorporating an existing space such as the dining room and not adding an extension at all. For your brief to be useful, you need to spell these kinds of thing out, with as much detail as you feel they need.

If you take the time and trouble to prepare a considered brief, it will give your project the best possible start. You will be able to approach the professionals with a confident idea of what you expect from them, and reduce the risks of wasted time due to misunderstandings.

Types of consultant

Anyone who is going to design and oversee your project should be carefully questioned and investigated, regardless of their formal qualifications. The main consultant that you will need to find is someone to prepare the design, specify the builder's work, and possibly manage the building contract on your behalf. Outside the construction industry, most people tend to refer to the person who fulfils this role as an 'architect'. In fact, there are various different types of people who design houses and house alterations, all with different types and levels of skill. As well as a designer, some projects may also need someone to advise on structural alterations, or someone to deal with tricky planning problems, or other professionals with specialist skills.

Architects

The title 'architect' is protected by law, and only designers who have completed a seven-year training course are allowed to use it. People who style themselves 'architectural consultants' or 'architectural designers' are not architects, and may not necessarily have any formal qualifications at all. An architect's training covers all aspects of the design and construction process, from small projects such as alterations to houses to large-scale buildings such as shopping centres.

All architects must be registered with the **Architects Registration Board** (ARB), an independent regulatory body set up by the government under the Architects Act 1997. Most architects also choose to be members of the **Royal Institute of British Architects** (RIBA), but this is not obligatory. If you need to check that someone using the title 'architect' is genuine, you can contact the Architects Registration Board (see Useful Contacts).

Technologists

Although their title is not protected by law in the same way as architects, these professionals are usually members of the **Chartered Institute of Architectural Technologists** (CIAT), which requires its members to be trained and qualified. (Note: this body was known as the British Institute of Architectural Technologists up until the middle of 2005). The training is shorter and less broad than it is for architects, but has a more practical edge. Aesthetic design skills are not considered essential to qualify, although some technologists develop these through experience.

Surveyors

Surveyors come in many different guises. Their background may be in selling houses, estimating quantities, building construction, or property management. Some can and do design houses, with their ability coming from experience rather than training. Again, the use of the title 'surveyor' is not protected, but most surveyors tend to be members of **The Royal Institution of Chartered Surveyors** (RICS), and have to have appropriate qualifications to do so.

Contractors

Some building contractors offer design services, although more often than not they subcontract this role. If you use them, it will always be on the condition that you are tied into using that builder for the construction work. You cannot expect independent advice from their designer, whose primary duty is to help the contractor, and you are prevented from inviting competitive prices from other contractors.

Unqualified designers

Just because someone lacks formal training or professional qualifications, it does not mean that they cannot do the job. However, you should investigate them much more thoroughly, to make sure that they have professional indemnity insurance (see later), and have acquired all the necessary skills to a competent standard.

Structural engineers

Current building regulations stipulate that any significant structural alterations must be assessed and specified by someone trained

Checklist of services offered by architects and designers

The following services are available from most architects. Some clients do not require the full service and, if so, the fees should reflect this.

Brief and site appraisal

Before starting work on a design, the architect has to assess the constraints and features of the site, existing buildings, and the client's needs and aspirations. It is also important to take a hard look at the budget.

Sketch design

Preparation of sketch designs, showing plans and the external appearances. From these sketches, a design is developed.

Planning Application

The architect will usually consult the local authority's planning department to assess whether your developing design is likely to gain planning permission. They then produce detailed drawings of your project, suitable for a planning application. This is the stage at which major decisions about the appearance of the house are taken.

Building Regulations

A Building Regulations application consists of a set of drawings, calculations and specifications describing the basic construction of your house. Your house has to conform to Building Regulations in order to be allowed to be built. Usually the architect prepares your Building Regulations application, submits it to the local authority, and deals with any queries that they raise.

Tender package

Drawings and specifications for tender are essential to obtain accurate prices from contractors. The drawings show the precise design and arrangement of the building components, and usually include details such as the stairs, fireplaces and internal fittings. A specification document shows the quality of both the materials and the construction. The fixtures and fittings are described in detail, stating the manufacturer and the specific component required.

Contractors

An architect can help you to find suitable contractors for your tender list, and see that the process of inviting tenders is carried out correctly. The architect can also prepare building contract documents before work commences.

On site

The architect can monitor the construction of your project. Regular visits are made to the site in order to check that the works are being carried out in accordance with the contract drawings, without any unnecessary delay, and in a professional, workmanlike manner.

Certificates

When a building society provides a mortgage for a self-build project, it may release the money at agreed stages of the work, on receipt of an architect's certificate. This certificate states that the building has been constructed to a satisfactory standard.

in structural design, and a submission for approval under the Building Regulations has to be accompanied by detailed structural calculations. A few other building professionals may have sufficient specialist knowledge for this work, but it is usually done by a qualified structural engineer. The title 'structural engineer' is not protected by law. To find a suitably qualified person, look for membership of the **Institution of Structural Engineers** (IStructE). This body requires academic training of, typically, three or four years, plus practical experience and the passing of further exams in order to achieve membership.

Quantity surveyors

The quantity surveyor's main role in a construction project is to monitor and control costs. Many QSs offer other skills and services, such as contract management. For the modest scale of house alterations, a budget estimate by a QS is unlikely to be cost-effective. For larger projects, such as a larger new house, their services can be invaluable, and contractors may not be prepared to submit tenders unless there is a **bill of quantities** available for them to price: this is an accurately measured list of the work and materials to be used in the building.

Planning consultants

For normal, uncontroversial domestic projects, the person who prepares your design is likely to deal with the local authority's planning department. If the planners refuse your planning application – or look likely to refuse it – and you can't negotiate a compromise, you may need specialist help in the form of a planning consultant. Most of these are members of the **Royal Town Planning Institute** (RTPI), which requires its members to have completed a relevant university degree and two years' practical experience.

Party wall surveyors

The Party Wall etc. Act is explained later in this book (see Chapter 5). If you have a dispute you may need one, two or even three separate party wall surveyors to sort it

out. Unfortunately, these consultants tend to be expensive, and are not easy to find.

Finding consultants

To start with, aim to come up with a shortlist of candidates, using some or all of the following methods:

- **Personal recommendation.** This is a good way to find anyone whom you need to provide a service, but many people do not often come across architects, or even know someone who has recently used one. If you encounter an architect at work, they may not be appropriate for your relatively small-scale project – although of course they may know someone who is.
- **Professional recommendation.** Consultants who work on similar projects tend to know each other. For example, an architect will usually be able to suggest the names of engineers and planning consultants with whom they have worked successfully before.
- **Professional bodies.** All the main professional organisations can put you in touch with their members in your area. (See the list at the back of the book.) They require their members to be qualified in various ways, and have professional standards that have to be complied with, including dealing with complaints, so membership indicates that a consultant has achieved a certain level of skill and professional conduct.
- *Yellow Pages* **and yell.com.** This is a useful starting point for many people; the problem is the sheer number of consultants listed, often with minimal information about them. Some of the professional organisations have separate boxes in Yellow Pages that list their members in the area covered. yell.com allows a search by postcode.
- **Other projects in progress.** There will probably be other building work going on near your site. Consider knocking on the door and asking the householders how it is going, and who helped them.
- **Local authorities.** The codes of practice

that planners and building control officers work to prohibit them from putting names forward. Some may give you an 'off the record' recommendation, but most will be uncomfortable doing this. However, the planning register is open for inspection and is available on the internet, via the local authority website in most cases. This lists the names and addresses of the agents who have submitted applications recently, so you can take a look at the drawings that they have submitted. This is an excellent way of building up a picture of the people you would be dealing with.

- **Magazines.** The magazines dedicated to domestic projects are filled with illustrations and case studies of projects, which usually give the names and contact details of the designers.
- **Others.** There are many other incidental ways of finding your ideal designer. There are several websites that claim to be able to help you, but it is important to check what designers have to do to get listed. If the answer is that all they do is pay a fee, there is little value to the recommendation.

Choosing the right consultant

Once you have a shortlist of consultants, you have to narrow it down to one. Naturally, you will want to do a bit of investigation, but the truth is it's your 'gut feeling' that counts the most.

- **Interviews.** First, be sure to spend a little time in the company of the person you are considering. The more crucial the consultant's role, the more you should find out about them before appointing them – as long as you don't take up too much of their time without paying for it.
- **Formal qualifications.** Ask some direct questions about their professional training and qualifications. If you don't understand what the letters after someone's name mean, it is perfectly reasonable to ask for them to be explained.

- **Experience.** Be prepared to ask some searching questions about the consultant's experience – or that of the consultant's practice. Do they work regularly with people like you, on your scale of project? If designers, do they have technical knowledge and competence as well as design flair? Some architects can be talented designers and artists who have never bothered much with the practicalities; the reverse can be equally true. Consultants who work on larger projects are used to being part of a large professional team, including other specialist consultants as well as their immediate colleagues. The budget for a modest extension, or even a whole house, can rarely afford this, so your consultant must be able to handle a wide range of problems alone, as well as having the sense to know when to call in specialist advice.
- **Architects.** Sometimes designers are accused of arrogance, and there are some like this, especially those who work on high-prestige commercial buildings, but the truth is that most architects are approachable, reasonable people; they would not be in business for long if they were not. Listen carefully to the way they answer your questions. Do you get straight, clear responses? One skill that is not included in an architect's formal training is the ability to listen – but it is an essential skill for them to possess if you are to work with them.
- **The size of the practice.** House alterations and one-off houses are usually best dealt with by small and medium-sized practices. Why? A large practice may not put priority on a minor project, and it may not be managed by anyone senior. An architect working on your project needs to communicate well with clients, anticipate and deal with problems efficiently, and manage fairly unsophisticated smaller building companies. So your project may receive less attention from a big practice than it requires. A smaller organisation will allow

you easy access to the directors or partners, who will at least be monitoring the project even if they are not working on it themselves.

- **Completed work.** Ask to see illustrations of previous jobs, and talk to past clients. Also, why not ask to see a set of drawings from an architect, or calculations from an engineer, for a typical project? You may be surprised at the range of quality and quantity of work that different consultants produce.

- **Indemnity insurance.** All professionals should maintain **professional indemnity insurance** (PII) to cover their work. Most of the professional bodies insist on it for their members. There is not the same compulsion on those who are unqualified, although if they are responsible people they will have it in place. If a serious error is made that costs you money, the benefit of that insurance is passed on to you – but you may have to go to law to get it!

Appointing a designer

The following points relate mainly to your architect or designer, but they apply to any consultant that you employ.

Paying a designer

Make sure you raise the question of fees and charges early on. Get a proper explanation of the fee structure, and of what you will get for your money, along with the payment terms, and expenses charged. Before you actually agree the fee arrangement, be sure that the appropriate level of services is being offered, and has been agreed and tied into the fee.

Designers may calculate fees by the hour, by a percentage of the build cost, or by a fixed fee (sometimes called a lump sum). The method used depends on how much information there is about your project, how much involvement the architect will have, and how the project is to be managed. For example, if there is no main contractor, then it is impossible to calculate a percentage of the contract value. At the beginning of a

project, it is unreasonable – and probably unwise – to expect a lump sum fee, because there is no way that the time required for the design can be accurately estimated.

Paying too little is as bad a mistake as paying too much, because the quality of service that you receive from your designer will influence the whole of the project.

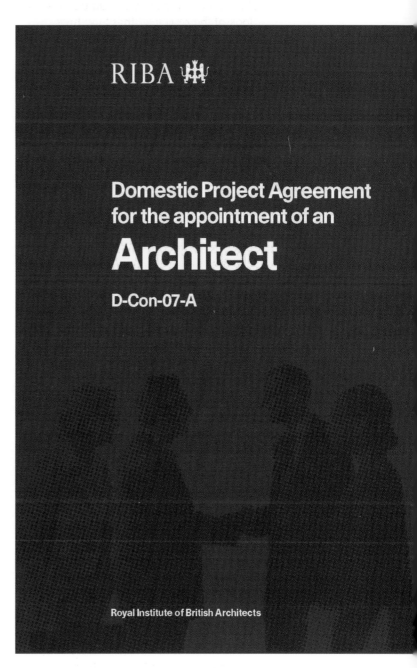

RIBA

Domestic Project Agreement for the appointment of an

Architect

D-Con-07-A

Royal Institute of British Architects

RIBA Domestic Project Agreement for the appointment of an Architect.

Appointment contract

Professional organisations such as the RIBA insist that their members have detailed written agreements with their clients, because it reduces the risk of misunderstandings, and ensures that clients are properly informed of their rights at the start of a project.

Some use standard appointment documents, such as those supplied by the RIBA, but others will want to use their own version. Do not accept a simple letter stating the fee. There should be a separate document detailing the services to be provided and the terms and conditions offered, which you should acknowledge in writing. If there is anything less than this, and something goes wrong, the absence of agreed terms and conditions could prove an expensive mistake.

A contract with an architect should cover at least the following issues:

- the exact level of service being commissioned
- which member of your family is to give the architect instructions
- who will be engaging other consultants, such as the engineer
- how fees are calculated, and whether VAT is due
- expenses, and how much they are (printing costs alone can be several hundred pounds for a large house)
- when you will be invoiced, and how long you will have to pay
- what happens if you are unhappy with something and don't wish to pay the amount invoiced
- how you can terminate the agreement, and what reasons you need to have to do this
- who owns the copyright in the design of your project
- if a dispute were to arise between you, how it would be settled
- who you can complain to if you feel that the required standards of professional conduct have not been met.

General principles

Planning laws exist to ensure that land is used properly and that development is appropriate, and to protect the environment. These aims are in everyone's interest – both nationally and locally. At the local level, the main aim is to protect the character and amenity of the area while allowing homeowners reasonable freedom to alter their property.

Planning legislation is complex and extensive. It is applied through the comprehensive and democratic local authority planning system.

Accordingly it is highly desirable to commission your design consultant to undertake the gaining of your planning consent.

When does planning apply?

Most development requires planning consent, although there are many kinds of alterations and extensions to houses that do not. If your project needs planning permission, and you proceed without the necessary consent, the consequences can be serious. You might have to remove the work, or get involved in costly and time-consuming litigation, which could subsequently affect the status and value of your property.

If you are thinking of altering your house, then always start by assuming that you will need planning approval. Contact the planning office at your local council with details of your proposed scheme, for their advice and formal confirmation on the need for planning consent or not.

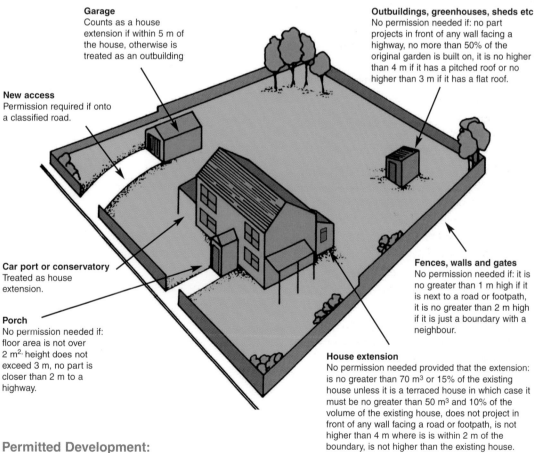

Garage
Counts as a house extension if within 5 m of the house, otherwise is treated as an outbuilding

Outbuildings, greenhouses, sheds etc
No permission needed if: no part projects in front of any wall facing a highway, no more than 50% of the original garden is built on, it is no higher than 4 m if it has a pitched roof or no higher than 3 m if it has a flat roof.

New access
Permission required if onto a classified road.

Car port or conservatory
Treated as house extension.

Porch
No permission needed if: floor area is not over 2 m², height does not exceed 3 m, no part is closer than 2 m to a highway.

Fences, walls and gates
No permission needed if: it is no greater than 1 m high if it is next to a road or footpath, it is no greater than 2 m high if it is just a boundary with a neighbour.

House extension
No permission needed provided that the extension: is no greater than 70 m³ or 15% of the existing house unless it is a terraced house in which case it must be no greater than 50 m³ and 10% of the volume of the existing house, does not project in front of any wall facing a road or footpath, is not higher than 4 m where is is within 2 m of the boundary, is not higher than the existing house.

Permitted Development: alterations to a private house that may not need planning approval.

These rules above may not apply if there is a listed building close by or the house is in an area of special control, such as a conservation area. Always check with your planning department or get professional advice if in any doubt.

For most household projects, the two main categories of work that do not need permission are:

- internal alterations, or works that do not affect the external appearance of the building
- permitted development (see below).

Permitted development

You do not need permission to alter or extend your house, or build outbuildings, if your plans fall within the permitted development allowances. There is only room to summarise these here; always make a detailed check with your local planning authority.

 Note: Most work carried out to a listed building, whether external or internal, will *always* require consent. Also, special controls apply if your home is in a Conservation Area, National Park, Area of Outstanding National Beauty, or The Norfolk Broads.

Sometimes a local council will remove the permitted development rights by issuing what is called an **Article 4 Direction.** This usually applies to conservation areas; it has also been increasingly applied to more modern housing developments.

You need to apply for planning permission for an extension to your house if:

- you want to build nearer to the highway than the nearest existing part of your house, unless there would be at least 20 m between your house (as extended) and the highway
- more than half the area around the original house would be covered by additions or other buildings
- the extension would be higher than the original house
- any part of the extension would be more than 4 m high and within 2 m of the boundary of your property
- for a terraced house, or any house in a Conservation Area, National Park, Area of Outstanding Natural Beauty, or The Broads, the volume of the original house

A sympathetically extended property (the extension the left half).

A house with an extension in a conservation area – special controls will apply.

would be increased by 15% or 50 m³ (whichever is the greater)
- for any other kind of house the volume of the original house would be increased by 15% or 70 m³ (whichever is the greater)
- in any case the volume of the original house would be increased by 115 m³.

Note: 'Original house' means the house as originally built, or as it was on 1 July 1948. Previous owners may have already altered the house. 'Highway' includes all public roads, footpaths, bridleways and byways.

You need to apply for planning permission for **roof works** to your house if:

- the work would make some part of the house higher than the existing roof
- a dormer window or other roof extension

would extend in front of the roof plane facing a highway
- the volume limits for extensions would be exceeded.

You need to apply for planning permission for a **porch** to your house if:

- it has a external plan area of more than 3 m²
- it is higher than 3 m above ground level
- it would be less than 2 m from a boundary with a highway.

You need to apply for planning permission for **detached buildings** and **other structures** on the land of your house if:

- the building or structure would be nearer the highway than your house, unless there is at least 20 m between the proposed building and the highway
- more than half of the area around your original house is already covered by buildings or extensions
- the building or structure would be more

Loft conversion under construction.

A porch reflecting the character of the house.

Note: Separate standards apply to **flats,** and usually planning permission is required for a wide range of works to such buildings.

than 3 m high, or 4 m high if it has a ridged roof
* the proposed building or structure is not for domestic use
* the building or structure would have a volume of more than 10 m³ if your house is a listed building, or is in a Conservation Area, National Park, an Area of Outstanding Natural Beauty, or The Broads.

Other rules apply to:

* fences, walls and fuel storage tanks
* engineering and other works to configure soil and gradients of the land
* vehicular access and hardstanding
* recladding
* aerials
* demolition
* conducting a business from your home.

Designing your scheme

It is advisable to follow the recommended consultation guidelines in Chapter 4 (Building control). Make a point of discussing your proposals with your neighbours; it is far better to sort out potential problems – to everyone's satisfaction – before they get dragged through the planning process.

Your local planning office can often offer guidance that will help to form the basis of a good design approach.

Making an application

When planning your project, allow enough time to prepare your application and get it approved. Planning law requires the planning authority to give a decision within eight weeks, but complex applications may well take longer than this. The planning authority often has to consult other relevant organisations, such as the parish council, highways authority, Environment Agency, or

A house with a new detached garage.

water company. It may also need to consult other council departments, such as environmental health or building control.

Most councils have special processes for dealing with minor householder works that can help streamline the process. These include householder guidance packs, design guidance, separate application forms, the delegation of decision-making to planning officers to avoid the need for involving the full planning committee, and hence quicker decision target deadlines.

Before you submit your application, always contact your local planning office for their advice on:

- whether an application is needed and, if so, what sort
- what application forms and other paperwork you have to complete
- what fees you have to pay
- what information you have to submit (plans, sections, elevations, and site and location plans)
- how many copies they require
- whether you need to alter your proposed design to smooth its path through the planning process.

Your application will be publicly advertised by some method: perhaps by a notice posted on your property, by post to your neighbours, or in local newspapers. The public have a right to comment on your proposal, but the planning authority will only take account of comments that are properly valid in planning terms. Even so, if they receive numerous 'complaints' this may well slow down the process.

Planning approvals

When the local planning authority has concluded its deliberations and everything is satisfactory they will send you an **approval notice.** Often approvals include conditions, usually to deal with standard matters of control. These may require you to submit certain aspects – for instance, a sample of your choice of bricks to be used – for further agreement.

Once your proposals are approved you may legally start work, subject to observing any conditions, and provided you gain any other necessary approvals. Note that building control approval is entirely separate from planning approval (see Chapter 4). Planning approval does not embrace building control, and vice versa. If both apply to your proposal you must make two separate applications and get two separate approvals.

Planning approval is normally valid for five years from the approval date. If you do not start work within that time your approval will expire.

You should of course build strictly in accordance with the approval and its conditions. If you subsequently want to alter the project in some way you must seek the amended approval of the planning authority.

Refusals and appeals

If your application is refused, or you do not agree with some of the conditions, discuss it with the planning office. Amendments may be advisable, and a modified submission might be acceptable.

The planning system has a comprehensive appeals procedure, and if you feel that a refusal, lack of decision or condition is unreasonable you may lodge a planning appeal. However, this is a potentially complicated and lengthy process, and it is always best to take expert advice before making an appeal.

Blankbourne District Council

Notice of Decision

Town and Country Planning Act 1990

Application submitted by :
Julian Owen Associates Architects
276 Queens Road
Beeston
Nottingham
NG9 2BD

Blankbourne District Council having considered an application

Applicant: Mr W R Wind
Development: 06/00123321/FUL
Location: Construct Rear Single Storey Extension
6 Flowers Avenue, Mustrum, Lancre NG15 0AB

as shown on the plans validly submitted ", HEREBY in pursuance of their powers under the above mentioned Act

GRANT PERMISSION

for the development as described in the application, subject to compliance with the Conditions imposed for the reasons set out below.

Conditions :

1.   The development hereby permitted shall be commenced not later than the expiration of three years beginning with the date of this permission.

2.   The new works shall be constructed using bricks and tiles of a type, texture and colour so as to match those of the existing building.

Reasons:

1.   To comply with S91 of the Town and Country Planning Act 1990 as amended by S51 of the Planning and Compulsory Purchase Act 2004.

2.   To ensure a satisfactory standard of external appearance and in accordance with the aims of Policies Env1 and Ho9 of the Blankbourne Local Plan (2008).

Summary of policies and of reasons for decision :

The proposal accords with Policies Env1 and Ho9 of the Blankbourne Local Plan 2008, and in the opinion of the Local Planning Authority there are no other material considerations which are of significant weight in reaching this decision.

Note to Applicant

This permission relates only to the scheme as amended by the revised drawings (Ref No: 1051/01 a, 03a & 06a) received by the Local Planning Authority on 8 & 12 January 2008.

Date: 28 January 2008

Authorised Officer

Planning Approval Notice

The Building Regulations

The Building Regulations are made under powers provided in the Building Act 1984, and apply in England and Wales. (Similar but separate regulations apply in Scotland and Northern Ireland.) They set standards to ensure people's health and safety in and around all types of building. They also provide for energy conservation, and inclusive access to and use of buildings.

When do they apply?

The Regulations apply when you:

- erect or re-erect a building or part of a building
- extend a building
- make alterations to the inside or outside of a building if they affect structural, fire safety, or disability matters
- convert a roof space
- re-cover roofs with a significant difference in structural loading
- underpin a building
- replace external windows or doors
- insert cavity insulation
- install an unvented hot water system
- replacing or renovating a 'thermal element' (i.e. the fabric of an external wall, roof or floor.

They also apply when you provide, extend or alter:

- washing and sanitary facilities and fittings
- sanitary pipework
- foul and rainwater drainage
- sewage treatment plants and cesspools
- boilers, flues, chimneys and hearths
- fuel storage installations
- hot water storage systems and controls
- electrical installations.

If any of these apply, then you must comply with the Regulations, and follow the building control procedures explained below.

The Regulations usually apply only to new work; they are not applied retrospectively to existing buildings. However, if the new work might adversely affect the compliance of the existing building, then you may have to

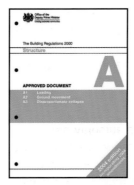

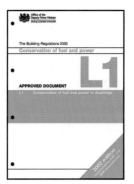
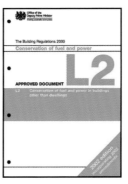

The Building Regulations consist of 18 Approved Documents.

upgrade it, or alter its fabric, layout or other arrangements.

The Building Regulations also apply to certain stipulated changes in the use of buildings, and in these cases can require the existing building to be upgraded to comply as if new, even if no actual building work is to be carried out. For residential premises this could include:

- creating a new dwelling
- creating a new flat
- creating a new 'room for residential purposes'
- altering the number of dwellings in a building
- converting an exempt building (see below) to a non-exempt use.

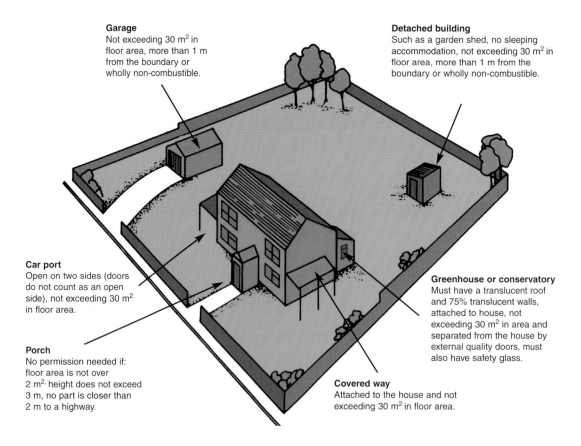

Garage
Not exceeding 30 m² in floor area, more than 1 m from the boundary or wholly non-combustible.

Detached building
Such as a garden shed, no sleeping accommodation, not exceeding 30 m² in floor area, more than 1 m from the boundary or wholly non-combustible.

Car port
Open on two sides (doors do not count as an open side), not exceeding 30 m² in floor area.

Greenhouse or conservatory
Must have a translucent roof and 75% translucent walls, attached to house, not exceeding 30 m² in area and separated from the house by external quality doors, must also have safety glass.

Porch
No permission needed if: floor area is not over 2 m²· height does not exceed 3 m, no part is closer than 2 m to a highway.

Covered way
Attached to the house and not exceeding 30 m² in floor area.

Alterations that may not require Building Regulations approval.

If you are not sure whether the Building Regulations apply to your intended project, you should seek clarification from the building control office at your local council.

When do they not apply?

Some standard domestic building works are exempt from the Building Regulations.

They do not apply if you **extend** a building at ground level by adding a conservatory, porch, covered yard or covered way, or carport open on at least two sides, provided the floor area of the extension does not exceed 30 m². However, if a conservatory or porch is wholly or partially glazed, the glazing must satisfy Part N of the Building Regulations ('Glazing – safety in relation to impact, opening and cleaning'). Any fixed electrical installation must satisfy Part P ('Electrical safety').

 Note: Conservatories must be substantially glazed, and be separated from the living accommodation by external-grade walling, doors and windows.

The Regulations do not apply to a **detached single-storey building,** if its floor area does not exceed 30 m², it contains no sleeping accommodation, and no point of it is less than 1 m from the boundary of the site, or it is constructed substantially of non-combustible material.

The Regulations do not apply to a detached building designed and intended to **shelter** people from the effects of nuclear, chemical or conventional weapons, and not used for any other purpose, if its floor area does not exceed 30 m^2; and the excavation for the building is no closer to any exposed part of another building or structure than a distance equal to the depth of the excavation plus 1 m.

They do not apply to a detached building with a floor area that does not exceed 15 m^2, and which contains no sleeping accommodation. This class of building includes smaller domestic **garages** and **garden sheds.**

Once again, if you are not sure whether your proposal is exempt, seek clarification from the building control office at your local council.

What do they cover?

The Building Regulations cover many different topics (see box). Some of these are large subject areas in their own right, such as structural stability, fire safety, and energy conservation; others may be more localised and have smaller-scaled detailed application. They are technical in nature, and frequently updated. So you should always seek professional advice on the design of your proposals and on whether they comply with the Building Regulations.

Approved Documents

The Building Regulations are worded simply, and set only broad performance requirements. For instance, Regulation F1 – Means of ventilation just says: 'There shall be adequate means of ventilation provided for people in the building.' This simplicity stops them from being too prescriptive, and allows for flexibility in complying with them.

To help people design and judge what is an acceptable standard of compliance with the core performance requirements, the government publishes **Approved Documents** in support of each of the technical Building Regulations.

These Approved Documents contain detailed guidance on how to comply, in the form of technical standards, codes of practice and references to other authoritative design guidance sources. If you

follow their guidance then you will comply with the legal Regulations. You do not have to follow them, but if you use an alternative approach you will have to convince the building control authority that you can achieve a standard at least equivalent to that referred to in the Approved Document.

Approved Documents are therefore important and useful sources of information. You can view or download them on the government website: www.planningportal.gov.uk/approveddocuments

Hard copies are published by NBS, and available from RIBA Bookshops Mail Order, 15 Bonhill Street, London EC2P 2EA tel: 020 7256 7222; e-mail: sales@ribabookshops.com; online: www.the buildingregs.com

The building control system

Anybody carrying out building work is responsible for complying with the Building Regulations. Under building control law the prime responsibility lies with the person responsible for carrying out the work, and for domestic work this normally means you, the homeowner. Other people involved, such as designers, builders and contractors, may also be responsible, and this is often linked in via their contractual and other liabilities.

There is a comprehensive, helpful and longstanding system used to administer the Building Regulations and related building laws. It is called building control, and it is operated primarily by building control surveyors based at your local council. There is also a private sector option available through the use of approved inspectors, who are private surveyors authorised by government to offer a building regulation service.

Local authorities administer and enforce the Building Regulations in their areas through the building control system. The process is intended to help everybody achieve compliance, and to prevent problems from occurring. The controls are normally applied via consultation advice, rolling, on-the-spot inspection of work, and accompanying guidance.

A thumbnail sketch of the Building Regulations

Part A – Structural stability

Requires buildings to be designed, constructed and altered so as to be structurally safe and robust against disproportionate collapse, and so as not to impair the stability of other buildings. Stipulates design codes to be adopted for use on all buildings, and also gives simple design rules for most masonry and timber elements for traditional domestic buildings.

Part B – Fire safety

Covers all precautionary measures needed to provide fire safety for building occupants, people near buildings, and fire fighters. Covers means of escape in case of fire, fire detection and warning systems, fire resistance of structural elements and building fabric, fire separation, protection, compartmentation and isolation to prevent fire spread and conflagration, control of flammable materials, and access and facilities for fire fighting.

Part C – Site preparation and resistance to contaminants and moisture

Covers site preparation, subsoil drainage, and measures to deal with contaminated land, radon, methane and all other site-related hazardous and dangerous substances. Also deals with weathertightness and watertightness of buildings, and the prevention of condensation.

Part D – Toxic substances

This controls the use of certain toxic materials in buildings.

Part E – Resistance to the passage of sound

Covers sound reduction standards between dwellings, for all new-build dwellings and the conversion of buildings to form dwellings. Sound testing may be required as a means to prove compliance. Also covers sound reduction standards between rooms used for residential purposes, and other acoustic controls of common areas in dwelling blocks and schools.

Part F – Ventilation

Sets out standards for the provision of ventilation and air quality for all buildings.

Part G – Hygiene

Lays down standards for sanitary and washing facilities, bathrooms and hot water provision. Also covers safety requirements for the use of unvented hot water systems.

Part H – Drainage and waste disposal

Requires adequate drainage systems to be provided, and deals with pollution prevention, sewage infrastructure, and maintenance and adoption regimes for sewers. Includes technical design standards for sanitary pipework, foul drainage, rainwater drainage and disposal, wastewater treatment and discharges, cesspools, and building over or close to public sewers. Also covers refuse disposal, and sets requirements for the storage and collection of solid waste.

Part J – Combustion appliances and fuel storage

Covers the construction, installation, commissioning and use of boilers, chimneys, flues, hearths and fuel storage installations, to control against fire sources, burning, pollution, carbon monoxide poisoning, etc.

Part K – Protection from falling, collision and impact

Sets standards for the safe use of stairways, ramps and ladders, plus requirements for balustrading, windows and vehicle barriers to prevent falling. Also includes requirements for the guarding of and warning of hazards from the use and position of doors and windows.

Part L – Energy conservation

Parts L1A and L1B are specific to dwellings. Part 1A sets out allowable carbon emission targets for new homes and the calculation methods to be used to ensure these targets are met. A blend of detailed controls are therefore exercised covering the insulation values of building elements and fabric, the extent of windows, doors and other openings, the air permeability of the structure, the efficiency of fuels used and of boilers together with their attendant heating and hot water systems, the commissioning of such systems, and also the efficiency of lighting and cooling systems. Prevention of undue solar overheating is also controlled.

The issue of Energy Certificates, operational instructions of systems and their controls and maintenance should also be produced.

Part L1B relates purely to the extension and alteration of existing dwellings. It includes some more simple 'elemental' rules of design based on minimum levels of fabric insulation and maximum allowable areas of window, doors and other openings.

Parts L2A and L2B relate to all buildings other than dwellings and as such it is outside the scope of this book.

Part M – Access to and use of buildings

Requires the inclusive provision of ease of access into and circulation within all buildings, together with requirements for facilities for disabled people. Does not apply to the extension of dwellings.

Part N – Glazing – safety in relation to impact, opening and cleaning

Covers the use of safety, or protected, glazing to avoid impact hazard; suitable awareness and definition of glazed areas; and safety requirements for the use, operation and cleaning of windows.

Part P – Electrical safety

Requires electrical installations within dwellings to be safely installed, tested and certified.

Regulation 7 – Materials and workmanship

Covers all materials, products, fittings and components, and requires them to be fit for their purpose. Also requires adequate workmanship to be applied in construction operations in order to achieve compliance in use. Sets out methods for verifying materials, products and construction methods via British and Euro Standards, CE marking, authorised testing and certification schemes.

There are two cornerstones to the system:

- applications for Building Regulation approval
- inspections of the work in progress.

However, there are stringent enforcement powers, which can be applied to persistent contraventions of work or procedures. Formal enforcement can be via criminal court proceedings to seek fines and have work altered or removed. Local authorities can also serve enforcement notices for contravening work to be altered or removed, or carry out remedial works themselves if necessary. Any person, including the local authority, can also seek a court injunction relating to any building regulation matter.

Building control powers relate purely to matters of statutory compliance; they do not cover contractual or consumer protection, or any personal preference aspects of your building scheme.

Documents required for a full Building Regulation application.

Making an application

Everyone planning to carry out applicable building works must make the appropriate Building Regulations application before work starts. It is an enforceable offence not to make such an application.

For household works, applications can be either **full plans** or **building notice.** For certain specialist installations, such as electrical works and boilers, accredited installers can self-certify their work if they are members of specified Competent Persons Schemes (see below).

The **full plans application** is the most traditional, reliable and widely used form of application. It consists in submitting details of your proposed building works to the building control office of your local council for pre-approval. The application usually comprises two copies of a simple application form, building plans of the proposal, and all relevant specifications, calculations and other supporting information.

The building control surveyor will then check these details, and comment on any defects or areas of query. If everything is satisfactory the council will issue an approval. This assures you that your scheme complies, and also joins the council in responsibility for the compliance of your proposals. Approval may sometimes be conditional, pending receipt of further information on specific issues.

The council normally has to give its decisions within five weeks of submission, although this can be extended to two months by mutual agreement. Normally they will give a technical response to applicants within two weeks of submission. So there should be enough time to resolve the application within normal timescales, but your project plan should always include an allowance for the time it will take to get approval: far better to receive the comfort of approval before you start work and get over-committed.

Sometimes applications are formally rejected. There may be an intractable problem, but normally it is just that the flow of necessary information has extended the timescale. In this case the process continues, and when all is resolved the application will be approved.

Many forms of household work can be conducted under a **building notice.** This is a simplified form of application, which can offer a fast-track route to planning your work. However, it should be used with care, because it offers no form of pre-check of the design, and no approval is given.

Basically it consists of submitting an application form that describes the intended work and, sometimes, site plans identifying the work's location. Usually the council does not require plans or details, but they may subsequently ask for proof of specific features of the scheme, such as structural or energy calculations. As there is no design check or approval of plans this method relies upon those carrying out the work to comply first time in order to avoid costly remedial alterations. So it is vital that everything is found satisfactory when the work is inspected, and that owners, builders and designers are totally confident of their own preplanning.

Building notices are probably not advisable for complex schemes, but they can offer advantages for minor or repetitive types of work. Another consideration is that councils are not obliged to give completion certificates (see below) for work carried out under building notices, although they do so where appropriate.

What does it cost?

Building Control is a chargeable service. Each council has a set scale of fees, and for householder works, depending on the types of work, these will normally be:

- taken from a general sliding scale, based on the cost of the work; or
- based on standard charges for various set sizes of domestic extension; or
- sometimes a mix of the two, if your scheme involves different works, e.g. an extension and separate alterations.

Fees are normally charged in two stages. A quarter of the total charge is payable upon submission of a full plans application (the **plan fee**), and the balance when the work starts (the **inspection fee**). If a building notice is submitted then the total fee must be paid up front. Applications are not valid until the necessary fee is paid. VAT is payable on all building control fees.

Competent Persons Schemes

This route to compliance with the Building Regulations can apply when specific stand-alone specialist works (such as replacement windows, electrical installations or boilers and flues) are carried out by installers registered under such a scheme (which has to be a scheme authorised by Government).

In this case you do not need to make an application to the council. The work is self-certified by the person doing the work, and the scheme operator issues a certificate to you and records are notified to the council for long-term property information purposes. It is the installer's or scheme operator's responsibility to give you all the certificates and pass the records on.

Avoiding problems

If your scheme contains any difficult aspects or uncertainties, the sooner they are dealt with, the better. It helps avoid costly, time-wasting mistakes and misunderstandings. Forestall problems before they arise, by consulting the building control surveyor for advice and guidance. This might be before you submit your application, during the course of the application, on site before construction, or even during construction.

For example, if you live in a sewered area, check whether there are any public sewers under or near where you wish to build, as their presence may seriously affect your proposal, or even prevent it altogether. Special approvals and conditions of building may be necessary. Establish the facts as soon you can, either by consulting the public sewer maps held by your local council, or by contacting your local water company, who are responsible for the public sewers.

Table 3 Competent Persons Schemes
The following works are covered by Competent Persons Schemes
Replacement Windows, Doors and Rooflights
Heat producing Gas Appliances and associated heating and Hot Water Systems
Combustion Appliances – Oil
Combustion Appliances – Solid Fuel
Electrical Installations
Plumbing, Heating Systems and Hot Water Systems (Dwellings)
Ventilation and Air conditioning (Dwellings)
Lighting Systems, Electric heating systems and associated controls
Air Pressure Testing of Buildings
CO2 Emission Rate Calculations
Sanitary Conveniences, washing facilities or Bathrooms in dwellings

For a current listing of registered Competent Persons Schemes and their contact points please refer to Government website: www.communities.gov.uk/index.asp?id=1131138

Loft under construction.

Loft conversions are a common form of improving and expanding your home, but they can face problems under the Building Regulations. This often relates to the need to ensure proper means of fire escape, particularly when the work will result in a house that is three storeys high or more. Also, the structural arrangements and sound insulation need careful design input and construction techniques. Always use an expert designer or installer for a loft conversion, and consult building control before you submit your application.

Planning

Building control approval is entirely separate from planning approval. Planning approval does not embrace building control approval, and vice versa. If both apply to your proposal you must make the two separate applications and get two separate approvals.

Inspections

Inspections are an important feature of the building control system. The building control surveyor inspects the work at various key stages, to check that the work conforms to Building Regulation standards. This also picks up any defects or potential problems, allows for solutions to be found, and ensures that any defects are put right.

The person carrying out the work must give **notice** to the council of each of these stages, as shown in the table. Often your builder will take responsibility for this, but you can also do it yourself; either way, you need to ensure that it is done.

Most building control offices aim to carry out the inspection the same day, provided they receive notice by an agreed time in the morning (usually 10.00 am).

Building control surveyors are empowered to inspect work at *any* stage, not just those covered by the statutory notice requirements. These are often equally important stages, which need to be inspected. You may want to agree with your builder and the building control surveyor an inspection framework tailored to the features of your particular works – to cover, for example, intermediate floor levels, party walls, roof structure, or any special structural arrangements.

Any **defects** discovered during construction must be dealt with. Similarly, any defects showing at completion must be remedied before building control will clear your work. Outstanding defects may attract enforcement action.

Table 4 Building control inspections: statutory notice requirements	
Commencement of work	48 hours' written notice must be given
Foundation excavations	24 hours' notice before concreting
Foundation concrete	24 hours' notice before covering
Oversite preparation	24 hours' notice before covering the fill and damp-proof membrane
Damp-proof course	24 hours before covering
Drains laid	24 hours before backfilling
Drains test	24 hours of test after backfilling
Occupation	5 days if to be occupied before completion
Completion	Maximum of 5 days after completion

NB: The above periods run from the end of the day on which the notice is given.

Work in progress.

Property records

When all the work is satisfactorily completed the building control authority issues a **completion certificate** confirming so far as possible that it complies with the Building Regulations. This is an important document. Make sure you get your work certified, and keep the certificate with your property records.

Documents recording the various statutory approvals, certificates and compliance have become vital property records that you will need to supply at various points of property transaction, and which will support the forthcoming **home information packs.** For example, formal legal searches are conducted on every house conveyance, and these include enquiries into the status and compliance of both current and previous building works.

Regularisation

If unauthorised works, i.e. works without approval, have been carried out, you can seek retrospective approval. This is called regularisation. Always refer to the local building control surveyor for discussion and advice.

Sustainable options

As you will have gathered the Building Regulations apply certain measures that will help the energy efficiency of your home to an extent. It is likely in the near future that they will incorporate further requirements looking towards the achievement of far higher sustainability targets.

In the meantime you may well feel that the time that you are doing works to your home is the best time to maximise on a range of possible additional range of sustainable approaches that could make a lasting improvement to your home.

Possibilities could include:

- providing thermal insulation values over and above building regulation standards to your walls, floors, roofs, windows and doors
- upgrading the insulation values of your existing structure in conjunction with your new works
- making your home more airtight, therefore stopping draughts and heat loss
- installing a new energy efficient boiler in lieu of any inefficient existing installation
- insulating your existing heating and hot water systems
- providing more sensitive controls to your systems
- move to low energy lighting
- generate your own energy by the possible use of: solar thermal panels – photo voltaic panels – ground heat pumps – wind turbine – hydro sources
- position porches, conservatories, winter gardens to avoid heat loss and gather solar gain
- use sustainable materials
- install water efficiency taps and fittings
- utilise rain water storage
- providing shading features.

Solutions do need to be tailored to each individual case and some of the suggestions need expert input. It is also advisable to

The contents of a Home Information Pack (HIP)

The following are some of the items that are listed in a Home Information Pack, for a freehold property

Standard enquiries of the local authority

Drainage and water enquiries

Mining search

Supplementary enquiries of the local authority

Contaminated land

Flood risk

Legal and Planning Issues

Summary of terms of sale

Fixtures and fittings form

Evidence of title

Sellers Property Information Form

Copies of warranties and guarantees relating to the building

Copies of any current planning applications

Copies of Building Control Certificates

Energy Performance Certificate

The Home's Energy Efficiency Rating, from A (good) to G (poor)

Environmental (CO2) Impact Rating

Summary of the home's energy performance related features – e.g, how well insulated the roof and walls are.

Recommended measures to improve the home's performance rating, graded according to cost.

keep a mind to the cost benefits that can be achieved from any set of proposals. However, it is often the case that real holistic improvements can be grasped at the time of doing improvements to your home.

Before you start

Very often, extensions and alterations to houses are on or close to boundaries or party walls. In these cases the lack of space can make design and construction tricky. Your scheme may well have a potential impact on your neighbours, and on their property. It may generate planning objections, make construction difficult and more expensive, or trigger the lengthy Party Wall Act process.

It is important to forestall potential difficulties, delays or disputes by assessing the situation early on. Before you commit yourself to a final scheme:

- Ensure there is an accurate survey and plan of the boundary lines and the linear and levels relationship to all features (including hidden services) on both sides of your boundary.
- Check that there are no legal ambiguities over boundary lines, rights or easements.
- Consider the impact of your proposal on the location (from both your point of view and that of third parties). Also consider the longer-term implications for access, maintenance and other future requirements.
- Check whether the Party Wall Act, or any other statutory controls or restraints, will apply.
- Assess whether there is sufficient access for the construction process over your own land, or whether access via adjoining land will be needed.
- Take advice from your designer and contractors, and from your solicitor if necessary.
- Consult with both planning and building control to ensure there are no fundamental design problems.
- Keep your neighbours informed, and discuss your plans with them.

This is just a summary; there are many different factors that can come into play. The box contains a more detailed checklist.

Once you have worked through this, you are equipped to develop your proposal in detail to accommodate any special features or programmes.

Boundaries

As long as you comply with statutory controls, and there are no restrictive covenants in force, you have a basic right to build on your property. Of course, in doing so you must not cause any damage to adjoining properties: this could attract common law liability. The construction process should always protect the integrity and rights of adjoining premises.

Boundaries can sometimes present legal problems. Boundary lines are not always well defined, and are sometimes not where physical features suggest they may be. Sometimes **easements** exist that allow rights of way, drainage or light across and between adjoining premises. If there are any uncertain legal aspects of the siting or effect of your building works, then you must consult a solicitor.

The Building Regulations allow for construction on or close to boundaries. They may impose special requirements – relating to foundation and structural stability, fire resistance, fire separation, sound insulation, or discharge of flues and chimneys, for example – but these can normally be readily achieved by normal construction specifications and techniques.

The planning process, quite rightly, exercises strict controls over proposals that significantly affect boundary conditions. This can relate to fundamental design issues such as:

- the mass and proportions of the new work in relation to adjoining buildings, and to your own
- good design features of your proposal
- control of undue overlooking
- maintenance of daylighting to adjoining properties
- the visual and spatial impact, such as the effect on the street scene, or maintenance of the gaps between houses.

Boundary and party wall checklist

- Survey and check boundaries and ascertain your legal demesne, your rights and any legal constraints.
- Visualise your proposal in terms of the impact on your property.
- Do the same for any impacts on your neighbours.
- Establish whether the Party Wall Act will apply.
- Consider the detailed design aspects of:
  - overhangs and aerial encroachments of structures and services
  - subsurface features such as foundation encroachments, the lines of services, any undermining of neighbouring buildings or land
  - discharge points of any existing or proposed flues, chimneys or ventilation openings, to ensure there is no overreaching or obstruction of discharge, and that there is sufficient isolation from the boundary to ensure unimpaired long-term function
  - maintenance of daylight to both properties
  - avoidance of overlooking
  - requirements for fire separation, such as non-combustible construction, or limitation of openings
  - weatherproofing at any abutments
  - any continuing need for access for maintenance, or accommodation purposes such as dustbins, or gardening
- Consider the planning situation, consult the planning authority, and establish acceptable planning criteria.
- Discuss with your contractor any special construction requirements, such as means of access.
- Give any notices required under the Party Wall Act, and reach agreements under that Act.
- Check that you have all legal and statutory approvals.
- Check that your contractor has an adequate construction plan that will avoid disruption or damage to your neighbours, such as undue noise, dust, debris, structural damage, or obstruction of access.
- Monitor the works to ensure that no unplanned problems occur in respect of the boundary condition.

It is always best to have professional design help in formulating your scheme and getting planning approval. This includes consulting the planning authority in advance, to ensure there will be no major problems.

Party walls

A party wall is:

- a wall astride the boundary, whether it separates two or more buildings, is purely part of one building, or is a 'party fence wall' (a wall that is not part of a building, such as a brick garden wall); or

- a wall wholly on one owner's land but which separates two or more owners' buildings.

The Party Wall etc. Act 1996 is an important and demanding Act, which allows for and protects the rights of all owners joined by a party wall. It establishes processes that should be followed by anyone carrying out or affected by works that:

- entail alterations directly to an existing party wall

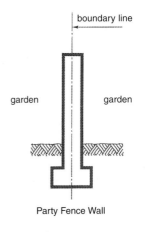

Party Fence Wall

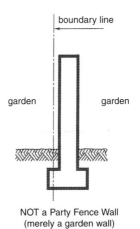

NOT a Party Fence Wall
(merely a garden wall)

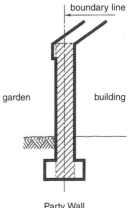

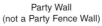

Party Wall
(not a Party Fence Wall)

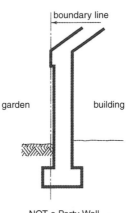

NOT a Party Wall

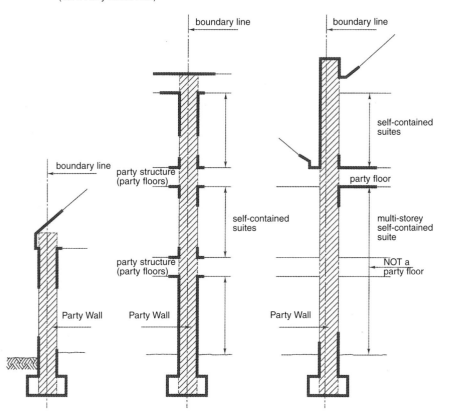

Definition of a Party Fence

'Party Fence Wall' as defined in Section 20 of the Act means a wall (not being part of a building) which separates the land of different owners, and which stands astride the boundary line.

Party Wall definition (a)

'Party Wall' as defined in Section 20 sub-section (a) of the Act means a wall which forms part of a building, and which stands on the lands of different owners, i.e. astride the boundary line (though not necessarily placed centrally).

Party Wall definition (b)

'Party Wall' as defined in Section 20 sub-section (b) of the Act means that portion of a wall which separates the buildings of different owners.

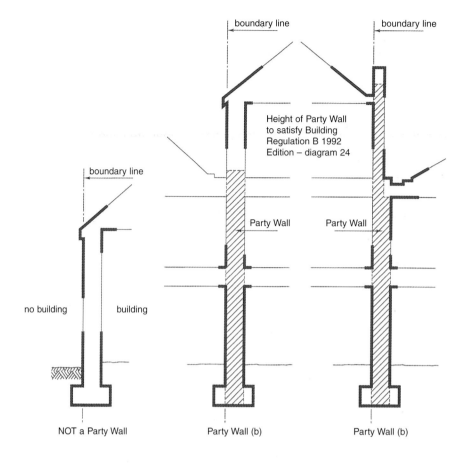

boundary line

boundary line

Height of Party Wall to satisfy Building Regulation B 1992 Edition – diagram 24

Party Wall   Party Wall

boundary line

no building   building

NOT a Party Wall   Party Wall (b)   Party Wall (b)

Application for 6 m and 3 m notices

Section 6 of the Act refers to the notices required in the event that the Building Owner proposes to carry out excavation or construction within a distance of 3 m or 6 m from an Adjoining Owner's building.

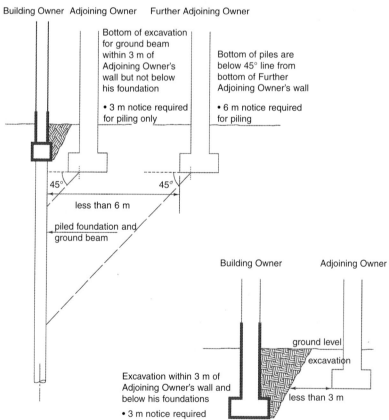

Building Owner Adjoining Owner   Further Adjoining Owner

Bottom of excavation for ground beam within 3 m of Adjoining Owner's wall but not below his foundation

• 3 m notice required for piling only

Bottom of piles are below 45° line from bottom of Further Adjoining Owner's wall

• 6 m notice required for piling

45°   45°

less than 6 m

piled foundation and ground beam

Building Owner   Adjoining Owner

ground level

excavation

Excavation within 3 m of Adjoining Owner's wall and below his foundations

• 3 m notice required

less than 3 m

- create a new party wall
- form excavations within 3 or 6 metres of a neighbouring building (see below).

Alterations to an existing party wall

If you wish to carry out various works to an existing party wall, you must give the adjoining owners two months' written notice of your intentions. They can then:

- give their consent in writing
- dissent from the work in writing
- within one month serve a counter notice outlining requirements for additional or modified work
- do nothing, which after 14 days of the serving of the notice constitutes a dispute.

If the adjoining owners do not give their consent, or reach agreement after discussion, the involved owners should jointly appoint an independent **agreed surveyor.**

The agreed surveyor will impartially draw up a **party wall award,** which takes account of the rights and interests of all the owners involved. It stipulates the works to be done, and how and when; apportions the cost of the work; make records of condition for monitoring purposes; attributes surveyor's fee payment; and allows for inspection of the work.

Work to form a new party wall

If you plan to build a new party wall astride the boundary, or wholly on your land but abutting the boundary, you must give one month's notice to the adjoining owners.

If, within 14 days, the adjoining owner agrees to the building of the wall, you may go ahead and start work after the one-month period has expired. All such agreements should be in writing, and cover the location and details of the wall, the allocation of costs and any other agreed conditions.

If the adjoining owner does not agree then you must build the wall wholly on your own land (but foundations of plain concrete may extend under your neighbour's land).

Alternatively, as before, an agreed surveyor may be appointed to formulate a party wall award.

Excavations near neighbouring buildings

This part of the Act applies when excavations and/or foundations are formed that are either:

- within 3 m of a neighbouring building, and extend deeper than the neighbouring foundations; or
- within 6 m of and will extend within a zone formed by a line struck down at 45° from the adjoining foundation.

If either situation applies then you must give one month's notice to the adjoining owner. They may agree in writing to the proposals within 14 days. If no agreement is reached then a dispute can be assumed and a party wall surveyor can be appointed to make an award.

Access

Neighbours must grant access for authorised works under the Act, and for supporting access for designing architects and surveyors. Also, any party wall surveyor appointed under the Act must be granted access.

The **Access to Neighbouring Land Act 1992** enables an owner to seek an access order from a court granting access onto adjoining land in order to carry out necessary work on his or her own land in the absence of any existing easement, wayleave or other consent. Access orders are likely to relate only to the need for reasonably necessary preservation works, and may be temporary, conditional and subject to compensation.

Enforcement

The Act is not administered by any enforcement agency, but it places responsibility under law on the owners who may be party to the proposed works. If the Act is not followed, any court proceedings will take the provisions of the Act into account.

Guidance

This has been only a brief summary of the Act. Always take professional advice if you are concerned about a particular aspect, or if you cannot reach simple and mutual agreement with your neighbours under the Act. Further guidance is available on the government website: www.communities.gov.uk/index.asp?id=1131402

Always consult your neighbours early on, to ensure awareness and agreement rather than confusion and dispute when they receive the formal notices.

Contacts for expert party wall surveyors can be obtained from The Royal Institution of Chartered Surveyors (www.rics.org).

Choosing your building contractor is probably the single most important decision you will have to make. The quality of the company you choose will determine the success of your project.

Do not believe everything that you read in the popular press or see on television concerning British builders. True, there are badly trained and dishonest people working in the industry, because anyone can set up as a builder without any qualifications or training. But the vast majority of builders are decent, honest people who take a pride in their work, and who will go to great lengths to satisfy their clients and protect their reputation.

The trick is to sort the wheat from the chaff. This will take some time and trouble, and you may need to lower your expectations as to the cost of the work and how quickly it can be started and finished.

When should you employ your builder?

There are several points in the project at which you may decide to appoint a builder: at the start; before there are any drawings; after you have received planning permission; after you have full plans approval under the Building Regulations; or once your designer has prepared a tender package. All these approaches have advantages and drawbacks.

You might engage the contractor at the start, for a complete **design and build** package. This has the benefit of providing a single point of responsibility and possibly a fixed price and programme at an early stage. However, it is difficult – and in some cases impossible – for them to accurately predict the cost of the work before proper drawings have been completed. The price will not be competitive. This is partly because, without thorough specifications and detailed drawings, you will not be able to compare prices between builders. The least reliable contractor may well quote the lowest price, because they will rely on adding lots of extras later as the design information becomes available, or they may

lower the quality of the work to ensure a profit. This is in sharp contrast to an honest, experienced company, which will include everything they know you are likely to want, and therefore quote a higher figure.

Another problem can arise when the price is left vague in the beginning. You may find that it has increased unreasonably later on, after the builder has produced the design and agreed the specification. Unless your contract expressly says anything different, if you wish to use the design that has been prepared, you are tied into using that contractor, at that price. You cannot use another builder unless you get a different design prepared. If you commission your own drawings directly, you can ask anyone to quote for the work and get reliable, competitive prices – you will pay for the design work one way or another anyway. Some contractors, who work to a high standard, have a good reputation and consequently are much in demand, refuse to tender for projects because their clients accept the extra cost in exchange for a guarantee of quality.

If you obtain prices after the **planning drawings** have been submitted, but before any construction drawings are prepared, it is easier to agree a price than with no drawings at all. Even so, many of the choices that affect the final cost are yet to be made. You will still have to allow the builder power to control the quality of the specification, or give scope for the price to rise once it is properly defined.

With a project of any complexity, the minimum information that should be prepared before agreeing a price consists of the Building Regulations full plans approval drawings, supplemented by extra details provided by the contractor that are necessary to calculate a price, but which are not required by the local authority (see box). A good illustration of the difference is provided by the bathroom fittings. The building control officer will want to be sure that the traps are deep enough, and that they are connected correctly to the drains,

Work that does not need describing fully or in detail for a Building Regulations application

- Manufacturers, suppliers and exact type of construction materials
- Exact dimensions of rooms and spaces
- Window and door quality, and manufacturers
- Ironmongery
- Specifications of fittings and fixtures, such as sanitaryware
- Radiator type and location
- Decorations and finishes
- Electrical sockets and switches, number and locations
- Plumbing layout and fitting design
- External works

but is not interested in the type, manufacturer or model of any of the fittings. Neither do you need to state the type of tap or its finish or whether the walls are tiled, but the choice of all these will greatly influence the cost of the work.

To get fixed prices, with a predetermined quality that you can control, all at cost-effective rates, you need to have a full set of drawings and specifications prepared by an independent architect.

Finding a good builder

There is an often quoted maxim in the building industry that says 'speed, quality and cost – you can have any two, but not all three'. There is a lot of truth in this: each of these aspects of building work is desirable,

but the client – you – must decide how to reconcile them. Building is an imperfect operation, and you will always need to make some compromises. Be realistic about the compromises you are prepared to accept, and then ensure that the workers on site know what you expect of them. The same principle applies to your choice of builder, as they will all have areas of weakness. For example, a builder who works to a high standard will not want to be rushed; a cheap builder will never be able to satisfy a client who expects flawless finishes.

At whatever stage you take on your builder, get at least three prices, and preferably more. A building contractor's decision on which projects to tender for is influenced by

What you may be looking for from a building contractor

- Cost-effective price
- Completion in good time
- Completion close to the date agreed
- An appropriate quality of workmanship
- Tidiness
- Courtesy
- Honesty

their workload, which can change overnight if they win another contract. So it is not unusual for a contractor to agree to tender one day, and change their mind the next. They may let you know, and send back the documents, but more likely they will either not submit a price, or else tender an unrealistically high figure. If they then get the job, it will have a big profit margin to compensate for the extra trouble. So a maximum number of contractors to approach initially, for an average two-storey extension is five, allowing for one or two to drop out along the way, or overprice. If you really must go to more, bear in mind that, if the tenderers find out, they may not bother to submit a price, because their chances of getting the work are greatly reduced.

So how do you *find* builders? Unlike most professions, builders are not licensed, which means that anyone with a mobile phone and a truck can advertise themselves as a builder. Unemployed DIY enthusiasts, firemen, funeral directors and software designers have all done just this, with mixed results. So, just as when choosing your professional advisers (Chapter 2), compile a list of likely firms and then whittle it down by a checking procedure. The trouble is, good contractors don't have to advertise – they get most of their work through personal

recommendation. The box lists some suitable places to start looking for building contractors.

Checking out building contractors

If you are going to hand your whole project over to one building contractor, it is crucial that you engage the right company, so you must apply some tough selection criteria. With the exception of choosing builders recommended personally by someone you know and trust, none of the methods listed in the box is reliable in itself, but together they can get you a reasonable shortlist to work with. The next stage is to carry out some basic checks, followed by a more detailed scrutiny of those who look like the best prospects.

First stage: a phone call

- **Can you easily get a full name and address?** If there is only a mobile phone number, and further details are not proffered immediately, cross them off straight away. The commonest reasons for such bashfulness are to hide from the taxman, from creditors or from unhappy clients. If they do give an address, is it their home, or do they have a yard and an office?
- **Membership of organisations.** There

First places to look for building contractors

Recommendations from friends, family and colleagues

Your architect

Yellow Pages

Local papers

Builders' merchants and product suppliers

Site boards by building sites

Internet sites that list contractors

Proactive contractors who mailshot after your planning application is submitted

Local authority planners and building control officers (strictly unofficially)

Local authority lists of approved contractors, which are sometimes available to the public

are a plethora of organisations for builders to join. Some require members to fulfil conditions; others just have a membership fee. There is a rule of thumb that says that the elaborateness of the logo is inversely proportionate to the value of the organisation: this is slightly unfair, but contains a germ of truth. The few professional organisations that individual builders may belong to include **The Royal Institution of Chartered Surveyors** (RICS) and the **Chartered Institute of Building** (CIOB). Another thing to look for with larger firms is an association with the organisation **ConstructionSkills** (formerly the **Construction Industry Training Board** (CITB)). This is the body that organises the training for the construction industry, and membership indicates a firm that is a certain size and has a commitment to the quality of their workforce. All the other builders' organisations, whatever grand claims they make about regulating their members, are effectively clubs for the benefit of their members. Despite high profile publicity campaigns by some of these organisations, when the crunch comes and there is a problem they tend to protect the interests of the builder who pays their subscription fees, rather than those of a disappointed customer. A few will even try to sell you insurance rather than ensure that you are choosing the right builder for your project. Membership of this type of organisation is not a guarantee of a good quality service.

- **Track record.** How long has their company been in existence? This is different from how long they have been in business. Some organisations have a habit of winding up their business one day and 'phoenixing' the next day by starting a new company with a similar name, and the same staff and offices. In this way they hope to avoid the debts and legal liabilities incurred by their previous incarnation. In fairness, though, small building companies are highly vulnerable to the bad payment practices

that are all too common in the industry, and occasionally are forced out of business through no fault of their own.

- **Staff.** How many permanent staff do they employ, as opposed to part-timers and contract workers? If their management team is one person, what happens when that person goes on holiday or is sick?

- **Availability.** Most good building contractors are booked up at least several months ahead. Some are booked up for 12 months by the end of the winter. So, if they are available next week, ask them why. Sometimes there is a genuine reason: typically, an expected contract has fallen through, leaving a sudden gap in their workload.

- **Behaviour and communication.** If the person you speak to doesn't listen properly, uses unnecessary jargon, or is evasive when asked straight questions, put a big question mark next to their company, and ask to talk to someone else if they are not in charge. If they make you uneasy in the space of a telephone call, think how you would feel after a six-month building project.

- **Readiness to quote.** Make it clear that you will require a fixed price, and will be using an industry-standard contract. If they are reluctant to provide a fixed price, consider crossing them off the list. They may start with a low price to get you interested but aim to make you pay far more by the end of the project. If they try to persuade you that you don't need a contract, bear in mind that decent contractors prefer a proper written contract for anything but the smallest project. If a builder suggests that you should use their own contract, get professional advice. The ones that are written in tiny grey letters on the back of a quote are usually heavily biased against their customers.

- **Builder versus architect.** Likewise, if they try to persuade you that you don't need an architect or other professional to inspect on your behalf, and that in this way you will save money, think carefully.

Some contractors prefer their clients not to have a source of independent advice, so that they are free to overcharge for extras and avoid quality control on site.

At the end of the phone call ask them to post you some information on their company, but do not be too disappointed if you receive little or nothing. Many building contractors who are excellent builders are hopeless at marketing, because it is not a necessary skill; as long as they have happy clients, there will always be work waiting to be done. Conversely, slick marketing brochures and flashy websites sometimes conceal a business that cannot get work any other way.

Once you have weeded out the dubious names on the list, you can move to the next stage and look more closely at the ones that are left. No contractor should make it on to your tender list unless you are sure that, based on what you know so far, you would use them if theirs was the most favourable tender. To save time you may leave some of the second-stage checks until after you have got prices back, but proper checks are essential before you commit yourself by signing a contract.

Second stage: research and visiting

- **Where do they work?** Insist on visiting their offices. If they won't invite you, find an excuse for a visit, no matter how brief. It is unlikely to be a palace, but you will get a good picture of who you are dealing with. If the office is based at home, the size of the house and make of car may tell you something about the profit margins the company works to.
- **References and portfolio.** When you go to see them, ask to see photos of examples of their work, find out where they are, and then ask for references. Visit the properties, and talk to the clients. A short chat will reveal more than written recommendations.
- **Insurance.** All building contractors must have public liability insurance and all the other insurances needed to run a construction site. It is acceptable to ask the contractor to confirm that these insurances are in place, and for what amounts. You can ask for actual documentary proof before you sign the contract.

- **Business management.** There are many ways to evade taxes and reduce costs by ignoring legislation. If a builder gives a wink and nod that you can save some money like this, do not use their services. If they are prepared to cheat the taxman, they may well cheat you too. The main reason why construction sites kill so many people every year is that employers like these fail to comply with the health and safety laws. You – or one of your family – could become one of those fatality statistics if you allow your builder to cut corners while working in your home.

- **Financial check.** For a relatively small sum you can access a report on any business, by using an Internet service, or one of the credit control companies. This will give information such as who the directors are and where they live, the turnover of the company, how long they have been in business, and their latest filed accounts. This information is easier to get if the company is limited. The more detail that you want to see, the more it costs: Companies House now charge only a few pounds for accessing this information online (www.companieshouse.gov.uk)

- **Payment terms.** Never pay significant amounts in advance. The accepted convention is to pay after work has been completed, or at agreed stages if the project runs for more than a couple of months (see Chapter 7). The exception is if there is a costly, bespoke item that has to be ordered from a manufacturer, such as a conservatory or timber frame. If a builder asks for a large up-front payment, do not take them on unless you are convinced that they have an exceptional, genuine reason and are not either going broke or planning to 'take the money and run'.

How to spot a cowboy

No business address

No proper telephone number

Use of logos on letterhead that they are not entitled to

History of regularly winding up companies

Immediate availability with no explanation

Poor standard of behaviour by staff

Reluctance to use standard contract

Reluctance to work with your professional team

Few or no previous clients to whom you can speak directly

No insurance certificates

Attempts to dodge tax

Unrealistically low quote

Demand for money 'up front'

Accompanied by a 'minder' wherever they go

Self-managing subcontractors

If you are not going to use a single main contractor, but wish to organise your own construction project, or if you just need a small amount of specialist building work (such as plumbing or plastering), you need a different tack to deal with the trades that you will employ. Some of the methods we have suggested for general contractors will work, but there are important differences. These people (and they are often just people, not businesses as such) are harder to find, and owe their true loyalty to their regular employers – the contractors who use them as part of a building team. They may not agree to a written contract, and any written record will probably have to be made by you. They will expect to be paid weekly, not in stages like a main contractor, and they will probably want cash. Often the only way to find out if they are any good is to actually take them on and sack them if you are unhappy.

It is a daunting task to get good workers, because even the established contractors complain that there are not enough reliable people around, and fewer and fewer young people are moving into the construction industry to replace the skilled older generation.

Many problems that develop with building projects can be traced back to the way the legal contract has been formed. People who allow work to start on site 'on a handshake' will only get through if luck is on their side, and they run the risk of losing both money and peace of mind if anything goes wrong.

Never agree to engage a main contractor for significant building work without a proper written contract from an independent source. You do not need to employ a solicitor to draft one especially for you; there are standard contracts that have been developed and agreed by committees made up from representatives from all the main bodies involved in the construction industry. They are fair to all sides, and are designed to anticipate the most likely problems and stipulate how they should be dealt with. On signing the contract, the employer (you) takes on certain duties, mainly concerned with payment, but also takes the ultimate responsibility for the contract, along with the associated risks. In this respect carrying out building work to your home is very different from buying something from a shop and being simply 'a customer'.

For a building contract to be properly set up, two elements have to be covered. One is the **contract** itself, which will include the information shown below. The other is as complete a description of the work as it is possible to make – the **contract documents.** Contractual disputes often develop as a result of gaps in this information at the time the contract was signed. If you have put the project out to tender, you should already have a reasonably detailed set of drawings and specifications. If you are employing a builder earlier in the process, and this level of information is not available when you sign up, make sure that the basis on which the builder has quoted the price and how extras will be agreed and calculated is crystal clear.

By far the best standard contracts available are those issued by the Joint Contracts Tribunal (JCT), an organisation that represents all the key parties involved in the

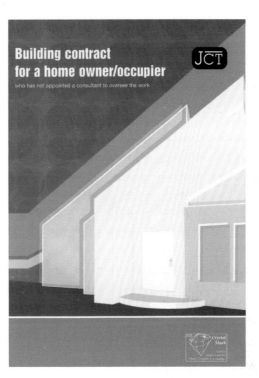

JCT Building Contract for a home owner/occupier.

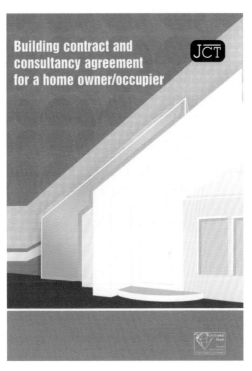

JCT Building Contract and Consultancy Agreement for a home owner/occupier.

JCT Minor Building Works Contract.

JCT Minor Building Works Contract with contractor's design.

building industry. The simplest one is called the *Building Contract for the Home Owner/Occupier.* It comes in two versions, one for when an architect or similar is used and one for when there is no independent consultant advising the client. It is for simple, straightforward house alteration projects, and is not suitable for larger projects, such as a whole new house. Unusually for a legal document, it has an award from the Plain English Campaign.

For projects of a bigger scale, JCT produces the *Minor Building Works Contract.* For work that is complex or costly, there are other contracts available, but none of these should be used without professional advice.

If you do not use one of these standard contracts, at least make sure that all the following points are recorded in writing.

The key terms of a building contract

- **The parties.** Who you are, and who the builder is. You may think this is obvious, but some builders have more than one company. Sometimes parties to contracts use the fact that they have been wrongly described in a contract to avoid their liabilities.
- **Identification of the works.** A brief description of the building work, such as 'Construct a two-storey extension to the side of No. 12 Letsby Avenue, Copton, Bedfordshire.' This is particularly important if the contractor takes on other work for you separate from this contract, such as landscaping.
- **The contract documents.** It is essential to state the specific drawings, by number and revision letter, as well as the version of the specification. These may be different from the tender documents if a price-cutting exercise has been carried out. They should be as comprehensive and unambiguous as possible. Sometimes it is just as important to state what the contractor is not expected to do. For example, if you employ a kitchen company, is the contractor to provide services capped off ready, or is it up to

the kitchen fitter to install the services? Who will lay the floor covering in the kitchen, and when?

- **Responsibilities.** If you are using an architect or similar professional to manage the contract on your behalf, you must make clear what authority they have. You should also have a matching, separate agreement with this contract manager. If there is not someone performing this role, and you are doing it, who takes on responsibilities such as dealing with the building control officer? Who out of your family will be the main point of contact? Who will keep a written record of any decisions made?

- **The tender sum.** This has to tie in directly with the contract documents, and must reflect any alterations agreed since the contractor first quoted.

- **Variations to the contract.** There should be a procedure for dealing with changes and how they will be identified and costed. If the contract documents have been properly drawn up, it should be relatively straightforward whether or not an extra is due, but it can still be difficult to arrive at a fair way of calculating the amount.

- **The project duration and liquidated damages.** Many of the problems that arise between client and builder are due to overruns. The contract should clearly state the time when work is to start, and when it is to be finished. A useful clause is one that states that any unwarranted delays will give you the right to deduct money from the payment due to the builder, usually a set amount for each

week. This amount must be a reasonable reflection of the costs to you that result from the delay, not just a high figure imposed as a penalty. The JCT Homeowner contract mentioned earlier does not have a liquidated damages clause and this would have to be added by adding your own amendment.

- **Payment terms.** Contractors are usually paid every four weeks, or at specific stages in the job, such as at damp-proof course level, or when the building is watertight. Also, a small amount is held back on each payment until the end of the job, usually 5%. A smaller amount is kept until 6 months after work is finished (usually 2.5%).

- **Insurance.** The contractor must have and maintain adequate insurance. But this will probably not be extended to cover items that belong exclusively to you and are stored on site, unless you ask for it.

- **Termination.** If either party has a reason to end the contract through no fault of the other, the contract should state procedure for doing this.

- **Solving disputes.** There should be a description of what the parties can do if there is a dispute, and what they have to do if it cannot be settled.

What if something goes wrong on site?

On any building project some things will not go according to plan. With careful planning, the right advice and a bit of luck, nothing serious will go wrong. But if it does, and you are at risk of being out of pocket, you will

---

Five golden rules for a building project

Never pay in advance except for specialist items

Agree amounts and dates for payment before work starts

Make regular visits to site for quality control

Always record key events in writing

Make the builder quote a completion date and try to hold him to it

need to take action. The best solution is to keep on speaking terms with everyone involved, and get the problem sorted out before you start to attach blame, and then try to negotiate a solution that involves the offending party compensating you in some way. The alternative might be to embark on legal action, which is far more lengthy and expensive, and should be a last resort. Ideally you should not embark on it before the work has been completed.

Unfortunately, the potential for things to go wrong with any building project is great, and the list of possible problems is a long one. However, rather than allow this to deter you from building at all, it is better to be aware of the risks, know how to reduce them, and know what to do if the worst happens.

Neighbours

The Party Wall Act was covered in detail in Chapter 5, but regardless of any legislation that is supposed to protect you, if you fall out with your neighbours, this may hinder building work. There are legal recourses available, but the truth is that it is rare for neighbours to be able to prevent building work once it has planning permission. The best you can do is be as diplomatic as possible, and keep them informed in advance of anything that may affect them. Don't resort to communicating only by letter; keep talking to them, however unpleasant it may get. Try to see it from their point of view: they will have to put up with a building site for several months, and may lose part of their view or a bit of sunlight from their garden. To sweeten the pill, you could get your contractor to do some maintenance work on their house.

Local and statutory authorities

If you have **planning approval,** and build in accordance with it, the planning officer should not bother you once work has started. It is worth someone checking that all the conditions written on the approval notice are being complied with – particularly those that ask for something to be done 'prior to the development commencing'. If

planners suspect that the height, footprint or location of the approved works have not been adhered to, they have been known to visit the site and take actual measurements to check that it has been built in accordance with the approved drawings. Ultimately they have the power to order incorrect work to be demolished if the problem cannot be resolved another way. Make sure that it is clear who is responsible for preparing accurate drawings, and who has to check that any changes are cleared with the planners before they are built.

Building control officers have a similar power to condemn work if it doesn't comply with the regulations. The difference is that the approved documents that describe their requirements are guidelines, and sometimes a compromise can be agreed. If you submit a full plans application and get it approved before work starts, and the builder is competent, there are unlikely to be significant difficulties.

Statutory authorities such as the water, gas and power providers have complex regulations that are only really understood by the specialist trades and designers. Make sure that anyone who works in these areas is properly qualified – something that is often demanded by the Building Regulations. Also check that there are no public or shared services running across your land. For example, you may not be allowed to build over a major public sewer, but can over a shared private one.

Health and Safety

The Construction Design and Management Regulations 2007 (CDM) look to ensure that good levels of health and safety at work are observed on construction sites. Your builder has a responsibility to build safely and comply with the CDM Regulations. He will need to preplan for this purpose and always make sure that workers or any other person on the site of the work, or in the vicinity, are not at risk.

As clients, private householders do not hold any direct responsibility under CDM.

Extras

Increases in cost once work has started are a notorious problem in the construction industry. Even the most sophisticated clients, such as government bodies, using top professionals for major buildings, can get into severe difficulties trying to control the budget. To reduce the risk of extras arising during your project, ensure that the information used by the contractor to quote is thorough. Even then, unexpected things can happen that no-one could have reasonably predicted. As long as there is a proper contract in place, which ensures that you are notified in advance and your approval is required before the extra work is carried out, you should at least be able to minimise the expense.

Delays

This is another classic problem for builders and clients alike. It is rare for a domestic building project to finish exactly on time. Allow a few weeks before the new furniture is booked to be delivered, or the carpet fitters are to arrive, and agree contingency plans should it become apparent that the overrun is going to be more than this. The contractor should be asked regularly whether or not they are on programme. Make it clear from day one that you are expecting completion on the date agreed. If your contract provides for liquidated damages (see above), it will allow you to deduct a realistic amount of money for each week the work takes beyond the contractual completion date. This is useful pressure to put on a contractor who seems to be too casual.

Quality control

As a domestic client, you are entitled to a competent standard of work, but also the work must be **fit for purpose** – in other words, regardless of how well or badly it has been built, the finished job must be suitable for the use that you intend for it. There should be checks in place during construction to ensure that the work is basically sound, such as regular meetings with the builders and inspections by a building control officer. If you have doubts, you can employ a professional adviser such as an architect to carry out inspections. It can be hard to define the acceptable level of finishes, though. A relaxed person's idea of a great job may look awful to someone who is more fastidious. If you are in the latter category, try to ensure that you get a contractor capable of achieving the required standard, and be prepared to pay for it.

Liquidation

If the contractor goes into liquidation in the middle of your job, the first thing you must do is make the site secure. Subcontractors and workers may attempt to offset their own losses by removing tools, materials or fixtures and fittings from the main contractor's sites. This is illegal, but common practice. If you have been paying the contractor in stages, and you have kept a retention back, this will help to reduce your losses. Some organisations that builders can join will compensate you, but only if you have specifically signed up and paid for their cover before work began, and if the builder is able to register as a member of a scheme. Credit checks, and looking for the warning signs mentioned earlier, will help reduce the risk of taking on a company that is financially unstable.

Design errors

If the design contains a clear mistake, the designer may be responsible rather than the builder, but it is sometimes not this straightforward. If the designer has been engaged only to obtain Building Regulations approval, and is not managing the project on site, then the contractor has the main responsibility to build it correctly and add any missing information. If a properly qualified architect is employed to produce a complete set of drawings and specifications this will reduce the risk of errors and mistakes.

Security

Building sites are targets for criminals. The security of the house is reduced, strangers are less likely to be challenged by neighbours, and valuable building materials, tools and equipment are sometimes left unattended. Experienced thieves will sometimes watch and wait until many of the fixtures have just been delivered, such as boilers, sanitary goods and furniture, before making their move. Simple precautions can be taken, such as putting temporary fencing around the garden and ensuring that workers board up the building securely before leaving for the day. It is vital that you inform your home contents insurers about the work before it starts. They will not agree to pay out after a burglary if you have not warned them of the increased risk.

Disputes with builders

If you are unhappy with your builder and end up in a dispute, bear in mind that it will be a major disaster for you if they walk out on the project, whatever they have got wrong up to this point. Unless you are dealing with extreme behaviour, such as blatant dishonesty or threats of violence, it may be wiser to accept a compromise. If possible, spare yourself the stress that results from having to fight a legal battle and having to find another contractor to finish the job. Many disputes arise because of genuine misunderstandings, or get inflated out of proportion because the arguments get personal and the people involved don't want to back down.

However, there are some instances where differences seem to be irreconcilable, and you will need professional help and legal advice. Get this as early as possible. You don't have to tell the contractor if you are still negotiating, and you may avoid making a procedural error that undermines your case. For example, if you deny the contractor access to the site and refuse to let them finish the work without following the procedure in the contract, you may lose the legal battle even if the contractor is proved to be at fault.

If you decide to hold back payment, make sure that you follow to the letter the rules set out in the contract. However distressing it gets, as long as you are not paying anyone in advance, and you keep back a retention from the contract value, you have the upper hand financially. Remember that the contractor has a lot to lose as well, and will be just as keen as you to set things right.

Your professional advisers

If you employ an architect or designer who is a member of an appropriate professional organisation, they must have professional indemnity insurance. If they make a serious mistake that costs you a significant amount of money, you can attempt to recover this and any closely related costs from them. However, it is the professional who is insured and not their clients, so you will have to prove that the mistake was clearly avoidable and the responsibility is theirs, at least in part.

If the designer is a member of a professional organisation such as the Royal Institute of British Architects, or is registered with the Architects' Registration Board, and you believe that unprofessional behaviour has occurred, you can make a formal complaint and it will be investigated. If negligence is proven the offending professional can be disciplined or even struck off, but these bodies do not have the power to award any compensation.

If you employ someone who is not a registered architect and not a member of a recognised professional body, the best that you can do apart from taking legal action is to complain to your local trading standards office, but they are unlikely to take any action except in the most extreme cases.

Legal recourse

If you wish to take some kind of legal action, the alternatives available to you may be decided by the contract you have signed. There is a 'quick fix' solution, called **adjudication,** which the Government imposes on all commercial building contracts. This involves an adjudicator reviewing the cases made by both sides over a 28-day period and reaching a temporary decision that is only binding unless and until it goes through a full legal tribunal, such as to court. However, the adjudication procedure is not imposed by the Government on contracts with private homeowners, so it will only apply if the contract specifically mentions it. Also, it is available to both parties, so the contractor can also use it to pressure the client.

If a full blown legal dispute arises, the contract may provide for it to go either to the **courts,** or to an **arbitrator.** Arbitration was conceived as a simpler procedure than going to court, although some experts feel it has become cumbersome, and that there is not much difference.

Some of the professional bodies offer **mediation** services, which try to resolve the dispute by discussion and conciliation, and this route is well worth trying if it is available and the other party will agree.

Mortgages

Most people purchasing a new home, or extending an existing one, will need financial support, usually in the form of a mortgage. The mortgage market is competitive, and you need to make sure you are getting the best deal. There are two basic types of mortgage. The first is the **repayment mortgage,** also referred to as a **capital and interest mortgage.** The monthly mortgage payment consists both of interest and of repayment of some of the capital (the money borrowed). In the early years the borrower pays off mainly interest but, as the mortgage reduces over the years, more of the monthly payment goes towards repayment of the capital. Although the capital reduces, the monthly mortgage repayments do not (provided the interest rate does not alter), so at the end of the mortgage term the borrower should have paid off the loan completely.

The second type is the **interest-only mortgage.** Here the borrower pays just the interest on the loan. There is no capital repayment element, so at the end of the mortgage term the borrower still owes the amount originally borrowed. This substantially reduces the monthly outlay, but it is only really suitable where the borrower has some method of repaying the loan, such as an investment that may grow sufficiently over the term to repay the capital. This could be life insurance, an investment portfolio or a pension plan, or a combination of any of these. If your income fluctuates, and there is a likelihood of large payments made to you, from an inheritance say, you can pay off the loan early – but check whether there are penalty payments for repaying the mortgage early (see below).

The basics

The **annual percentage rate** (APR) is the basic figure you should consider when receiving offers from a mortgage company. This is the figure that all lenders must provide, as it indicates the cost of borrowing, allowing for any fees that apply

and how often the interest rate is calculated (that is, whether daily, monthly or annually). The APR normally varies from the actual interest rate quoted. For an example, a lender might offer a mortgage of 6.6%, but the loan has an APR of 6.8%.

The other basic item of information is the **mortgage term**, which is, simply, the period over which you take the loan.

Repayment schemes

Once you have selected your mortgage, the lenders will offer you various options for repayment, as listed below.

- **Flexible mortgage.** This is where you have a mortgage facility agreed up to a specific sum, or percentage value of your property, and you can increase or reduce the monthly repayments, or even have a payment holiday to suit your specific circumstances. This flexibility means that you can make a higher monthly payment, or pay off lump sums, thus reducing the mortgage term. This type of loan normally carries a cheque book facility so that you can draw additional funds up to the agreed facility level to finance alternative purchases, such as a car, or perhaps to pay off credit cards. The advantage is that, as the loan is secured against your property, the interest rate will normally be lower than that offered by hire purchase or credit card borrowing. Also, the interest on this type of loan is normally calculated on a daily basis.
- **Variable rate.** Here the interest rate offered by the lender is variable, and so, although it is set at a particular rate at the outset, it will fluctuate throughout the mortgage term. Rates can go up or down.
- **Discounted rate.** This is a variable rate with a discount for a specified period, but the rate still increases or reduces in line with the variable rate to which the loan is linked. For example, if the variable rate is 7.5% and you have a discounted mortgage of 2% for two years, the payment rate during this period will be 5.5%. If the variable rate increases

during the discounted period by 1%, the payment rate will increase to 6.5%. Normally, at the end of the discounted period, the rate reverts to the variable rate.

- **Fixed rate.** Here the lender offers a fixed rate of interest. This is normally set for a specified period of time. For example, a rate set at 6.5% for three years means that the repayment rate is fixed during this period, irrespective of any fluctuations in the lender's normal rate. So even if the variable rate increases to, say, 9.5% or goes down to 3.5%, you will still be paying the rate of 6.5%. Normally, at the end of any fixed period, the rate reverts to the variable rate.

- **Capped rate.** This is a variable rate loan that is guaranteed not to increase above the capped rate offered by the lender for a specific period. Normally, at the end of any capped period, the rate reverts to the variable rate.

- **Cashback.** Here you receive a payment on completion of the mortgage – either a fixed amount or a percentage of the mortgage amount. For example, some lenders offer a cashback loan at the normal variable rate as an alternative to a discount rate.

Redemption penalty

This is a penalty that the lender imposes if you repay the mortgage loan in full or in part during the term of the loan. When you take out a mortgage, it is important to find out what the redemption penalties are. Many lenders do not now charge an early redemption penalty if you borrow at the lender's full variable rate. However, if you accept a discounted rate, you may find that there are penalties if the loan is repaid early.

Arrangement fee or administration fee

If you are arranging your loan through a mortgage broker there may be a specific arrangement fee payable to the broker. The broker should declare their level of fees to you in writing before arranging any mortgage on your behalf.

Some lenders also charge an arrangement fee. Depending on the lender, this may have to be paid in advance, and generally it is not refundable if you do not proceed with the loan application.

Insurances

We strongly recommend that you seek professional advice regarding adequate life insurance and sickness and health insurance, and this is dealt with in more detail below.

Insurance

As the owner of a new house, you will have to consider certain types of insurance cover, as listed below.

Buildings insurance

If you purchase a freehold property, your lender will insist that you take out insurance to cover the building in respect of damage caused to it. Costs vary between insurance companies, and you should obtain competitive quotations. Most lenders will encourage you to place the insurance through them, although they will normally allow you to insure with a company of your choice, but be aware that some lenders charge an administration fee to check your insurance arrangement.

With a leasehold property, such as apartments, the freeholder insures the property, and each leaseholder pays a proportion of the buildings insurance to the freeholder each year. If you are purchasing a leasehold property, ensure that buildings insurance has been arranged on your behalf.

Contents insurance

It is not compulsory to insure the contents of your home, but we strongly recommend it. Most people arrange their contents cover with the same insurer as that for the buildings, and this has certain advantages, although it is possible to arrange separate policies for buildings and contents.

All risks

There are various add-on extensions to the basic insurance policies, and you should seek professional advice from an insurer or broker when arranging these, which cover such things such as jewellery, pedal cycles, caravans and boats.

Life insurance

We strongly recommend that you arrange sufficient life insurance to pay off the mortgage in the event of the demise of any of the owners of the property. Insurances can also be arranged to provide a lump sum in the event of the owners being unable to work because of illness or injury. Obtain professional advice from insurance companies or brokers to ensure that adequate protection is in place to cover you and your family.

Warranties

New housing

Most of the warranties available today are concerned with new housing. The driving force behind the requirement for a warranty is with the lending institutions and many banks or building societies will require a warranty for any new-build dwelling prior to lending funds to the development.

There are four key names in the new housing market place who will supply a warranty; NHBC is perhaps the best known together with Zurich Building Guarantees. Other providers include Building Life Plans whose policy is underwritten by Allianze and Premier Guarantee who use the services of a Lloyds syndicate to insure their warranty.

These warranties offer a ten year insurance which is generally all encompassing for the fist two years of the term. The insurance will then reduce for the remaining eight years and will often only cover major structural damage or water penetration of the building envelope. All of the insurances differ however and you would be best advised to seek individual quotations and information from each provider prior to making any purchase.

The building warranty market is regulated by the Financial Services Authority who operate a complaints procedure for anyone unhappy with the operation or procedures associated with warranty.

Home extension or refurbishment

With the establishment of the new homes warranty market above it was inevitable that the market would extend into the home extension arena. This market was not driven by the lenders however but by the trade associations run by the builders themselves. Recognising that warranties provide security for the home owner the trade associations started to offer ten year insurance backed warranties for home extensions and alterations.

Conservatories – A Complete Guide

Julian Owen

Crowood Press Ltd

ISBN-13: 978-1 86126 726 9

A detailed guide to the planning, managing and completing of a conservatory.

Do It With an Architect

Barbara Weiss and Louis Hellman

Mitchell Beazley

ISBN-13: 978-1 84000 194 5

An excellent and humorous guide to getting the best out of your architect.

Self Build: Design and Build Your Own Home

Julian Owen

RIBA Enterprises

ISBN-13: 978-1 859 46139 6

A book in similar style by the author of this book.

Home Extension Design

Julian Owen

RIBA Enterprises

ISBN: 978-1 85946 248 5

Describes the process of altering or adding to a home in detail, with advice on how to introduce a high quality of design.

The Housebuilder's Bible

Mark Brinkley

Ovolo Publishing Ltd

ISBN-13: 978-0 9524852 4 7

This covers many of the practical issues, with detailed and updated guidance on building costs.

The Gaia Natural House Book

David Pearson

Gaia Books Ltd

ISBN-13: 978-1 8567 5196 4

An excellent book for anyone interested in sustainable or 'green' building and designing for healthy living.

House Plus

Phyllis Richardson

Thames and Hudson

ISBN-13: 978-0 500 34211 4

A lavishly illustrated book full of good ideas for altering private houses, particularly for modern or contemporary design.

The Sunday Telegraph Guide to Looking After Your Property

Jeff Howell

Macmillan

ISBN-13: 978-1 405 04658 9

One of the best books on the alteration and repair of houses ever written. Sensible, informed advice on every page.

Getting The Builders In

Paul Grimaldi

Elliot Right Way Books

ISBN-13: 978-0 716 03012 6

Useful tips on how to select, appoint and manage building contractors for alterations to your house.

Architects Registration Board (ARB)

8 Weymouth Street, London W1W 5BU

Tel: 020 7580 5861

Fax: 020 7436 5269

Email: info@arb.org.uk

Website: http://www.arb.org.uk/

British Board of Agrément (BBA)

PO Box 195, Bucknalls Lane, Garston, Watford, Herts WD25 9BA

Tel: 01923 665300

Fax: 01923 665301

Website: www.bbacerts.co.uk

Chartered Institute of Architectural Technologists (CIAT)

397 City Road, London EC1V 1NH

Tel: 020 7278 2206

Fax: 020 7837 3194

Website: www.biat.org.uk/

Chartered Institute of Building (CIOB)

Englemere, Kings Ride, Ascot, Berkshire SL5 7TB

Tel: 01344 630700

Fax: 01344 630777

Website: www.ciob.org.uk/ciob/

ConstructionSkills

ConstructionSkills, Bircham Newton, Kings Lynn, Norfolk PE31 6RH

Tel: 01485 577577

Fax: 01485 577793

Email: information.centre@citb.co.uk

Website: www.citb.co.uk/

Council for Registered Gas Installers (CORGI)

1 Elmwood, Chineham Park, Crockford Lane, Basingstoke, Hants RG24 8WG

Tel: 0870 401 2200

Fax: 0870 401 2600

Email: enquiries@corgi-gas.com

Website: www.corgi-gas-safety.com

ELECSA Ltd

44–48 Borough High Street, London SE1 1XB

Tel: 0870 749 0080

Fax: 0870 749 0085

Email: enquiries@elecsa.org.uk

Website: www.elecsa.org.uk

Federation of Master Builders (FMB)

Gordon Fisher House, 14–15 Great James Street, London WC1N 3DP

Tel: 020 7242 7583

Website: www.fmb.org.uk

Fenestration Self-Assessment Scheme (FENSA Limited)

44–48 Borough High Street, London SE1 1XB

Tel: 0870 780 2028

Fax: 020 7407 8307

Email:enquiries@fensa.org.uk

Website: www.fensa.org.uk

Heating Equipment Testing and Approval Scheme (HETAS)

Secretary: J M Lake, PO Box 37, Bishops Cleeve, Cheltenham, Glos GL52 9TB

Tel: 01242 673257

Fax: 01242 673463

Website: www.hetas.co.uk

Institution of Structural Engineers (IStructE)

11 Upper Belgrave Street, London SW1X 8BH

Tel: 020 7235 4535

Fax: 020 7235 4294

Website: www.istructe.org.uk

Local Authority building Control (LABC)

Website: www.competentperson.co.uk

National Association of Professional Inspectors and Testers

The Gardeners Lodge, Pleasley Vale Business Park, Mansfield, Nottinghamshire NG19 8RL

Tel: 0870 4441392

Fax: 0870 4441427

Email: info@napit.org.uk

National House-Building Council (NHBC)

Buildmark House, Chiltern Avenue, Amersham, Bucks HP6 5AP

Tel: 01494 735363/735369

National Inspection Council for Electrical Installation Contracting (NICEIC)

Vintage House, 37 Albert Embankment, London SE1 7UJ

Tel: 020 7564 2323

Fax: 020 7564 2370

Oil Firing Technical Association (OFTEC)

Foxwood House, Dobbs Lane, Kesgrave, Ipswich IP5 2QQ

Tel: 0845 65 85 080

Fax: 0845 65 85 181

Website: www.oftec.org.uk

Royal Institute of British Architects (RIBA)

66 Portland Place, London W1B 1AD

Tel: 020 7580 5533

Fax +44 (0)20 7255 1541

Email: info@inst.riba.org

Website: http://www.riba.org

Royal Institution of Chartered Surveyors (RICS)

RICS Contact Centre, Surveyor Court, Westwood Way, Coventry CV4 8JE

Tel: 0870 333 1600/020 7222 7000

Fax: 020 7334 3811

Email: contactrics@rics.org

Website: www.rics.org

Royal Town Planning Institute (RTPI)

41 Botolph Lane, London, EC3R 8DL

Tel: 020 7929 9494

Fax: 020 7929 9490

Website: www.rtpi.org.uk

The Stationery Office Bookshop

Tel: 0870 600 5533;

Email: book.orders@tso.co.uk

Website: www.tso.co.uk/bookshop